DIRECTING

BASICS

40 Questions
40 Answers
54 Executions

40 years in film production by William Irish.

Fifty years of communication
experience described in a book
that contains the how-to's of
film direction, forty questions
and answers on the subject of
directing and forty-fife true stories
about production and executions.
Written and illustrated by an
award winning veteran of Canada's
communication industry.

FriesenPress

Suite 300 – 852 Fort Street
Victoria, BC, Canada V8W 1H8
www.friesenpress.com

ISBN
978-1-4602-5009-9 (Hardcover)
978-1-4602-5010-5 (Paperback)
978-1-4602-5011-2 (eBook)

1. Performing Arts, Television, Direction & Production

Distributed to the trade by The Ingram Book Company

This book is dedicated to
my amazing partner,
Kathryn Elizabeth Irish.

ENJOY!

Preface

Directors are storytellers.

The purpose of this book is to provide those who choose to try their hand at directing
with tools to ensure their stories will be understood.

Feature directors must have knowledge of the basics of film construction
and have demonstrated abilities, somewhere in the world, of feature production.

Documentary directors must have knowledge of the basics of film construction
and have deep interest and knowledge of the subjects they shoot.

Commercial directors must have knowledge of the basics of film construction
and a well developed knowledge of marketing.

Table of Contents

Film Basics include

Definitions - pages 1 and 2

Eye Lines - pages 3 to 5

Continuity - page 4

Cutting - pages 7 and 8

Framing - page 9

Marketing - pages 12 to 15

Table of Contents for

Student questions & the author's answers - page 18

Table of Contents for

Production stories - page 49

Shot Definitions

A common language for ease of communication.

A WIDE SHOT is commonly used as a MASTER SHOT.

A MASTER SHOT holds all the action in a scene.

Directors usually begin with the MASTER SHOT because it takes the longest to light and covers all of the activities in a scene.   When the director needs to know just where everyone was and where the light was coming from in his closer shots, he reviews the master and retrieves the details he needs.

A MEDIUM SHOT shows details the viewer couldn't see in the wide shot.

A CLOSE UP shows the viewer something they couldn't see in the medium shot.

A MACRO SHOT or a TIGHT SHOT is a detail the viewer must see to help the story make sense.

A MICRO SHOT is an item that has to be magnified before it can be seen.

The images captured up to now tell most of the story of Harry's murder. The wagon came down the road and we saw Robert knock Harry out of the wagon and under the steel-rimmed wheels. Robert swore Harry had never been in his wagon but a fellow on a hill beside the road had seen the whole thing and a button from Harry's shirt was found in a corner of Robert's wagon. Perhaps a microscope spotted a virus on Harry's shirt that was also on Robert's sleeve and it aided the investigation and made a tight case.

If this was your story, you would have told a clear and understandable tale with a MASTER WIDE SHOT, a MEDIUM SHOT, a CLOSE UP and a MACRO SHOT.

The sun is setting and it is going to rain tomorrow but a key to your story remains undone. You need a medium or a close up to identify the man on the hill.

The director and the cameraman review the master shot. They are reminded of the stance of the man on the hill, how sunlight fell on him and what the objects are that should surround him. The shot is lit in a nearby tent or shed, objects are placed in the right relationship with the performer, and the director informs the actor as to the direction of his line of sight or EYE LINE.

When an EYE LINE is not correct, the viewer is confused and the director proves he does not know his craft.

Eye Lines

The EYE LINES of performers never look directly into the camera.
If they do, that action makes the *camera* a person in the story.

When a woman watches her friend pick flowers,
and the two are on the same level, the EYELINE
of the viewer must be level.

When a swordsman is dying on the ground, the
EYELINE of the observer must angle downwards
towards the dying swordsman.

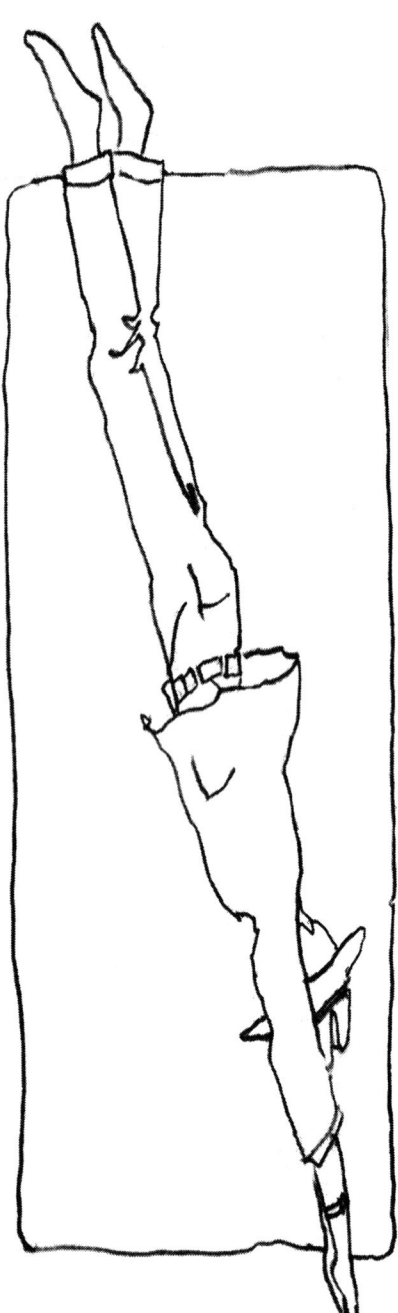

If a fully dressed man pops up in the middle of the lake and does not look at the camera, we assume he is alone.

If he dove into the water with a jacket on and rose up out of the water without a jacket and is still wearing his hat,

we have Continuity problems.

If, in the shot following his appearance in the lake, his clothes are suddenly dryer than they should be and there is a mustard stain on his hat, the director and crew are not paying attention.

On a professional shoot, at the beginning of a scene, the script person carefully photographs and notes each item worn by the performers. After lunch, the script person checks for mustard stains and notices the swimmer's watch is missing and his shirt does not have all the wrinkles it should have if it dried inside his jacket - hence continuity.

Eyeline Directions

The Rules of Direction will ensure your viewer's understanding.

The way to avoid confusion in an interaction between anything with eyes is to draw an imaginary LINE between the two participants.and stay on one side of the LINE for the two shots that show each side of the interaction.

The imaginary line

The woman on the left speaks to the woman on the right who answers her. If you have kept your cameras on the same side of the imaginary line, your viewer will not have any difficulty in understanding what is going on.

If one of the cameras crosses the imaginary line, your viewer will need a wide shot to show them what the situation is. Until the situation is clarified, your viewer will wonder why these two women are not looking at each other. Confusion will distract your viewer.

Two men sitting on a park bench chatting and looking at the lake, rather than at each other, need a MEDIUM SHOT to show the viewer what the situation is.

Question.

How does the LINE work when there is a larger number of participants?

Answer.

The director shoots a MASTER then shoots a tighter shot for the close-ups of the selected participants and draws a LINE between them. For each of the subsequent people speaking to each other, another LINE is drawn. During the group conversation, a performer may change from looking camera left to looking camera right because the director wants to add someone else to the conversation. Since the switch was seen on camera, the director can now shoot from the other side of his LINE until it changes again. The person speaking may also change focus to include all of the people in the conversation, and this frees the director to go where he wants or to cut to a wider shot.

If our viewer is to know who is doing what to whom in a scene containing two fighters, a LINE must be drawn and re-drawn for each feature of the fight. If the information the director needs to convey is the moment Jack slugs Bobby on the jaw, the director draws a LINE between the two and stays on one side of the LINE. A long fight might need a lot of LINES, for a lot of moments the director wants to see, but all those LINES are required if the director is to convey to the viewer exactly what happens. For complex fights in feature films, there are fight specialists who can get the job done faster than a director who is inexperienced in the genre.

Cutting

The director's job is to provide the editor with shots that tell the story, shots that can speed up or slow down the story and shots that can be used to create the emotional moments of the story. If the director gives the editor the wide shot only, he tells the story but there is only one way to cut it. If the director gives the editor a variety of shots, the editor will have many ways to stitch the story together.

The director can save time in the story by implying that something is happening.

When a man and a woman are walking in the same direction in adjacent shots, it is implied that he is either following her or going to the same place.

When the warriors riding left to right are cut next to warriors riding right to left, we imply the two are going to meet, and as the story continues, we find out.

In the late 1920's, Russian director Sergi Eisenstein, engaged in experiments on the implications of both frame design and shot relationships. He noted that the lines of Japanese Haiku were similar to a shot list and when the lines were changed to a series of images, the group conveyed both their rational meaning and an emotional quality.

An evening breeze blows
the water ripples
Against the Blue Heron's legs
Buson

Three images cut together
give us an emotional effect.

Trans Canada Telephone sent my crew to Prince Edward Island to shoot a moment during which two young lovers said goodbye. It was a normal, rational piece of film that told the story clearly. Then the editor and the writer decided they would spend the last fifteen seconds of the sixty-second commercial on nothing but waving reeds and a distant train whistle. The end result reminded me of a Haiku poem.

A gentle kiss
wind in the reeds
the howl of a lonely train.
Takasaki

Three shots cut together
give us a tender moment.

In his experiments, Mr. Eisenstein took a single inexpressive face and placed it adjacent to a flower, a lion, a storm and a butchered animal. In every case, the viewers read the inexpressive face as feeling emotions that were relevant to the shot adjacent to them.

The placement of subjects in the frame and which shots are placed
adjacent to them, direct and affect the viewer's emotions.

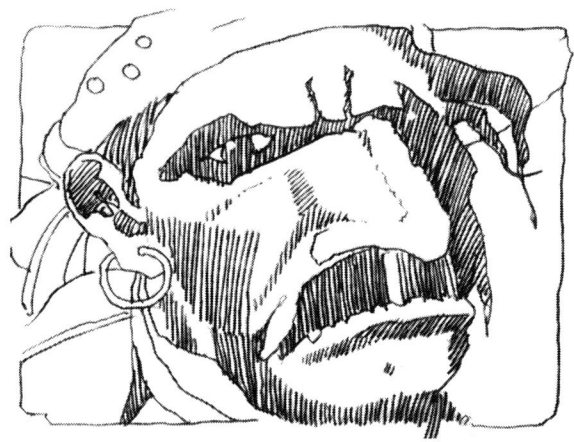

The manner in which you place the objects in your

Frame

and how they are placed in relation to adjacent shots,
affect the viewer's emotional response.

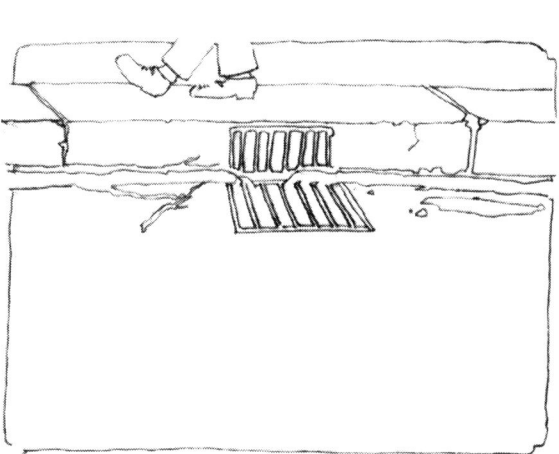

How you choose to use framing is part of your signature as a director.

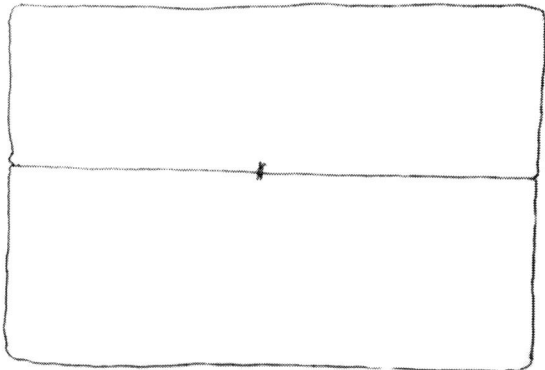

Lawrence of Arabia.

9.

Now you know how to:

Identify your shots,
avoid confusing your viewer,
look professional
and are aware
that your film's visual and emotional
language is yours to invent.

Now is a good time to view
some classics and films you admire.

Each kind of directing requires its own body of knowledge.

DOCUMENTARY DIRECTING
requires a deep interest in, and knowledge of, each subject.

FEATURE DIRECTING
requires a knowledge of dramatics, the film industry,
how to manage large spaces of time
and very large amounts of money.

COMMERCIAL DIRECTING
requires a knowledge of
film basics and marketing.

Commercial examples will be used to demonstrate
other parts and skills of directing because the author's
experience is principally in commercial direction.

MARKETING

We live in a free market society.
Anyone who chooses to sell or promote a product, service, politician or idea
within the limits of our legal system, may do so.
Lies, cons, self-agrandizement, gross exaggerations and prejudicial remarks are
made public, shunned and fined.

All participants, including directors who want to take part in the sale of
a product, service, political view or idea,
need to know all of the pieces that are included in the process.

The steps in the MARKETING process are:

1. acquiring the knowledge of a public need
2. researching solutions for that need
3. finding who has the need and where they live
4. inventing a solution to the need
5. costing the parts of the solution
6. assessing levels of competition
7. designing the area for distribution
8. testing product solutions
9. designing promotional solutions
10. producing promotional solutions
11. assessing the degree of success.

Numbers 1 to 8 are undertaken by the manufacturer or provider.

Number 9 takes place with the assistance and skills of an advertising agency.

Number 10, if the promotional solution is visual,
is produced by a film production house (which plants and grows directors).

Number 11 is done by the agency or is outsourced to a research agency.

What is an Advertising Agency?

Please note - The need for a director doesn't kick
into the marketing process until stage #10.

The activities of stage #9, take place in an advertising agency where experienced
marketing managers guide a *Creative Department* in their invention of
communicating solutions for the product. The *Creative Department* consists of a Creative
Director and groups of writers partnered with art directors. A good Agency

employs good *creatives*. The ability to invent is not however limited to the *Creative
Department.* Good ideas pop up in all Agency departments.

Advertising Agency storyboard that was sent to the Production House.

Brian Mulroney's government was having difficulty funding Air Canada. He and his
political advisors decided to remove the expense by selling the airline to the public.
See *Share our Tomorrows* - williamirish.info - The title implied *"buy our shares."*

What is a Film Production House?

When the Agency creative group finds a solution that answers the product's needs and the solution is a commercial, they illustrate their idea as an Agency storyboard and work it through communication, comprehension and attention tests until it is approved by the manufacturer's marketing team. Once approved, the marketing team calls for directors' reels and quotes from film production houses. Directors from several production houses are chosen and asked for their opinions which they express in a director's treatment storyboard. After reviewing the director treatments, the creative group chooses a director. The following was the treatment board for Prime Minister Brian Mulroney's *Share Our Tomorrows.*

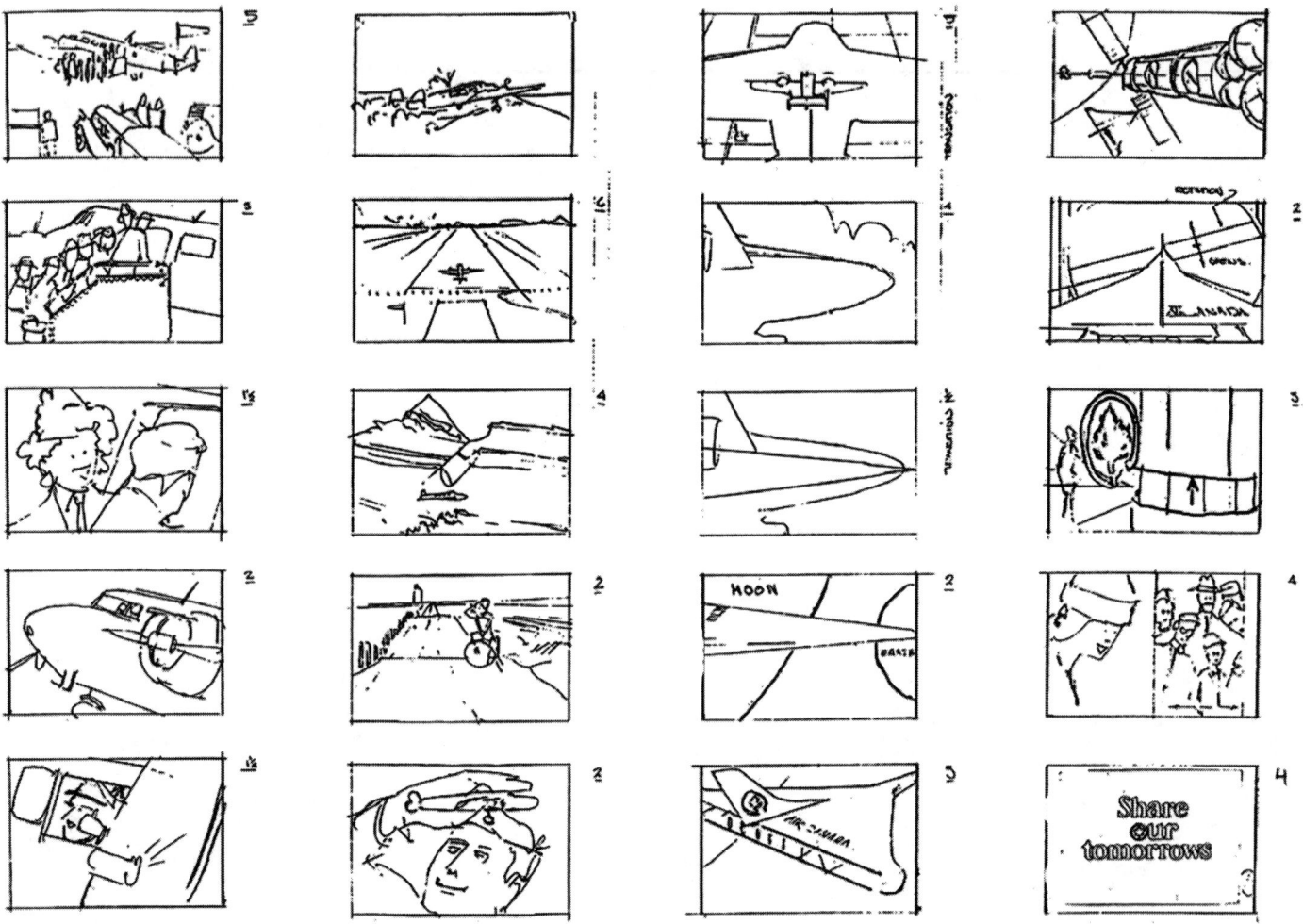

For some reason the Prime Minister was in a great hurry. The drawing above is the overnight treatment done in a rush and faxed back to Foster Advertising the following morning for approval. Word of the appointment came in the afternoon. The director was on an Air Canada flight to Calgary the next morning.

The completed commercial is at williamirish.info and a full story in the blogs, page 53.

**Different corporate structures have different marketing procedures.
General Foods had a clear and simple system.**

**A product designated *GREEN* meant the product was new and unknown and
should be promoted with clear information of its use and advantages.
A product designated *YELLOW* meant the product had reached maturity.
Advertise the product's advantages and help it make as much money as it can.
A product past maturity was said to be in the *RED zone*
which meant the product was dead.
Spend nothing on it and use the money it earns to develop a new product.**

So how does this relate to directing?

If the director receives a storyboard for a *green product,*
his job is to make the product information as easily understood as possible.

If a *yellow product* has strong competitors,
the director's job is to emphasize the product's advantage
over its competition.
The director's invention is allowed and often appreciated when he
finds ways to place emphasis on minimal differences.

Directors do not need to worry about the *red zone.*
Storyboards are not drawn for products in the red zone.

**The General Foods example
is a good one to keep in your mind
as you approach all products.**

Directing has moments of elation and moments of difficulty.

If you want to direct commercials in order to eventually direct feature films, you may
succeed but few do. Even though the directing skills are similar,
the body of knowledge required for each is different.

If you seek fame and riches, you will not do well.

If you are looking for a craft in which to become skilled
and are willing to work cooperatively with others,
you will be financially well cared for and have at least fifteen minutes of fame.

Visit a film studio before you commit and watch some commercial shoots.

When you visit a commercial shoot, you will see that you have on the studio floor, a
corporate marketing person, the Agency Art Director and Writer, the Agency
Producer and the director's studio producer.

A commercial director is not the boss. He is a person full of
knowledge, a master negotiator, gentle, and a member of a team.

If he builds a reputation for commercials that do their job well,
his job becomes easier and his fee increases as more people
are willing to listen to what he has to say.

The position of successful director is earned not gifted.

Q&A

I was asked to share my 40 years of experience as a director
of commercial film with the students of a local college.
Public speaking was not a practiced ability
so I gave the students
a sheet of paper with this request.
"Tell me what you would like to know."

They complied with vigour and the answers to their questions
kept us going one day a week for two months.

Their questions and my answers follow.

Questions

page 19. How did you learn to direct?

page 19. Do you make good money as a director?

page 20. Why did you pick this industry?

page 20. What is the busiest area in Canada for commercial production?

page 20. What kind of commercial production were you involved with?

page 20. Do you have any tips for beginners?

page 21. What was your specialty?

page 21. How would I begin a business as a director?

page 21. Please explain the jobs of producer and director.

page 22. How closely does a director work with his crew and technical people?

page 25. Was the Tempra commercial scripted?

page 25. Who creates the idea for a commercial?

page 28. What is the best way to direct talent?

page 29. What process is used for creating an original idea?

page 30. Are you a freelance director or do you work from a production house?

page 30. Have you had a good idea then had it stolen?

page 31. How do you go about making a commercial?

page 34. How do you decide what to shoot?

page 34. Have you ever done a commercial the client was unhappy with?

page 35. Is working with children difficult?

page 35. What is the story behind the Air Canada commercial?

page 36. How do you inspire talent?

page 37. Have you ever had a vision from which the end result strayed?

page 39. What insight can you give me for working in the industry?

page 40. When your crew becomes unmotivated, how do you re-motivate them?

page 40. Do you get to pick your own crew?

page 41. Do you have a choice of the commercials you do?

page 42. Have you worked in countries other than Canada?

page 43. What was your worst directing experience?

page 43. Have you met a lot of famous people?

page 44. Do you ever create your own scripts?

page 44. Do ideas change between the office and the shoot?

page 45. What is done on a field survey?

page 45. How much control does the director have on the choice of talent?

page 46. Have you ever made a commercial for a product you didn't like?

page 47. Did you have any training as a director?

page 47. Has there ever been a simultaneous video recording done of one of your shoots?

Q. How did you learn how to direct?

A. Over the course of seven years I fell into directing by following my interests.

First art school, which gave me samples of work so I could apply for a job as an art director in an advertising agency. Art school was followed by photography in a photo studio and finally as a support person in a film studio. The film studio put me in a place where I could watch how commercial directing was done, ask questions and look for answers.

Q. Do you make good money as a director?

$$$$$$$$$$$$$

A. Let's assume you do what I did. When I was sure I was useful to the film studio, I asked permission to come in at 4.00 a.m., before the studio opened, borrow a camera and shoot a still life situation. The studio recognized there was a benefit to the studio if I could shoot something of value. I produced a reel of five still life situations and because they approved of my work, the studio put my name out as a skilled shooter of still life. I earned a small amount more for the still life work than I did as a support person. After several successful jobs, my next still life became one with people sitting at a table and I I Iwas sold or advertised as someone who could direct vignettes. I was now paid about the same as a plumber (not bad). Another studio saw me as an inexpensive employee with promise, so they hired me to direct full commercials. I was paid the standard rate of the novice, $3,000 a shooting day. Three shooting days a year left room for part-time jobs. Eventually work came in from Quebec. A snowmobile company represented by McKim Montreal, liked my reel and wanted a spot that explained their machine was tougher than anyone else's. The cinematographer suffered a concussion, a sprained leg, a broken right arm and an unchanged cinematographer's salary. The spot won the year's best commercial award and I suffered a substantial raise in *my* daily rate. Top American commercial directors earned up to $30,000 a shoot day. At that time, top Canadian commercial directors earned on average, $15,000 for a day's work. Ridley Scott progressed from commercials to feature films and now earns unspeakable but appropriate amounts for his contribution. Directors are usually paid only for their time on the studio floor, not for their preparation work or their time at the water fountain.

After the shoot, everyone sits in front of a screen and views the product of the shoot day. If approved, the footage is given to the editor and he produces one or ten final cuts which again everyone views.

ADVICE - Work for subsistance amounts to get started.

Q. Why did you pick this industry?

A. I didn't. I approved of the idea of a free market where anyone could bring their product to a buyer's attention, any way they could, within the limits of the law. During my time in advertising agencies, I was challenged to invent, *write and draw,* ads and commercials that gave consumers the information my client needed them to hear. My work as an art director pointed out to me that I didn't know as much as I should about photography. I decided to go into a photography studio to learn and passed through that into a film studio because my curiosity pushed me in that direction.

Q. What is the busiest area in Canada for commercial production?

A. Commercial production in Canada grows where industries construct products. Most industries and their advertising agencies are in Toronto, Montreal, Vancouver, Calgary and Winnipeg.

Q. What kind of commercial production were you involved with?

A. Troubles arose in the second film production company I worked for. The manager who was good at his job asked seven people in various positions at Rabko, to join him in a new company. The seven, myself included, agreed and Partners Film Company was formed. I saw my place in that company as *a "general practitioner"* and accepted almost all jobs offered to me, which meant I did not specialize. I did cars, trucks, oil, soaps, cereals, cosmetics, churches, politicians, snack packs, fast food restaurants, gas stations and many more things I can't think of at the moment. You name it, I was probably fortunate enough to have worked on it. I was generally not chosen for commercials where music was a principal issue because I am tone deaf.

Q. Do you have any tips for beginners?

A1. A beginner does not have the same skills as an experienced director. The experienced director will steal all the jobs because he is well known and well promoted. A senior's runs around $15,000 a shoot day. The first thing an Agency does when there is a job to put out, is to ask for reels (samples of a director's work). As a junior, if you have a good reel and are willing to work for $3,000 a shoot day, you have a chance to beat out an experienced director. The Agency assesses the relevance of your skills and the depth of the risk in using you. If the film studio sells you on the basis that you will redo anything you mess up, you are on your way. Your reel should carry ONLY your best work.

A2. It helps if you can bring other skills or preferences to the job, such as mechanical engineer, artist, writer, fashion designer, cosmetics, still photographer, marketer, electronics etc. Your natural interests will colour and polish the product you produce.

Q. What was your specialty?

A. Interests that helped me succeed as a "general practitioner" were visual skills, Agency experience and the marketing knowledge I picked up along the way.

Q. How would I begin a business as a director?

A. Wait and gain experience. Watch other directors. Read. Make your move into business after you have learned how others have failed and after you have gathered base financial resources. Consider adding equal partners who can broaden the character of your business. When one director is not the flavour of the week, another one will be.

I have seen only one person who was popular the day he began. He was an art director who wore gum boots to work and disliked deodorants. His employer was Young and Rubicam. He called in all the Toronto directors' reels and studied them for three weeks. At the end of that time, he claimed to be a director. He was successful and ended up as a director of grand and exotic moments in England.

Another art director, from a Seattle, Washington agency plopped into Toronto with a job for a new type of French fries. Our company quoted and I got the job. In the middle of the shoot, before lunch, the man lost his temper over something none of us understood. He screamed and wailed and seemed to be directing his anger at me. He turned out to be a man who had pulled this stunt several times, a stunt designed to frighten the director into quiting. He would then take up the position of director, finish the commercial, put it on his reel and collect the director's fee. In my case, I was fortunate to have a crew who were loyal. As soon as he started to scream, the crew left, leaving him without the tools to finish the job. This method of becoming a director is not recommended.

Q. Please explain the jobs of director and producer.

A. A *director* of commercials is responsible for selling a treatment for the commercial that is in accordance with the Agency's objectives. After he fully understands the Agency objectives, he draws a director's treatment, writes a shot list, specifies locations or set construction, set-dressing and chooses the talent in cooperation with the Agency writer, creative director and art director. He informs his camera person about what he will be asked to do on the day and shows him who is where, and what the performers are going to do. On the shoot day, the director and camera person work very closely together. If the size or complexity of the shoot warrants an added cost, the director is given one or more assistant directors.

There are three producers on a shoot: an Agency producer who oversees the production, a production house executive producer who quotes and supervises costs, and a production house producer, who oversees the shoot. The production house producer sees to it that all of the parts covered fit the budget, ensures the right number of bodies get to the right places and have the resources they require. Production house producers do most of the production work. They cover the needs of the talent unions and fill sudden gaps to save the day.

Q. How closely does the director work with his technical and film crew?

A. I was very fortunate. When I joined the commercial film studio, I brought with me a man who had worked as an assistant cinematographer and now wished to be upgraded to cinematographer. After a few jobs, the management took a dislike to him, let him go and teamed me up with a fellow who had a lot of good work behind him. One of his earlier jobs as an assistant cinematographer had been to prepare, load and maintain 36 large cameras that were mounted on a steel frame and lowered out of the bomb-bay doors of a Lancaster bomber. The job of the bomber was to photograph 360 degrees of Canadian countryside for an International Exhibition. The cinematographer's name was George Morita and his knowledge of cameras and the needs of his job were extensive. When Mr. Morita discovered I often did not know what to do next, he made his extensive knowledge available to me. His generosity and my admiration for his skills made us friends. I brought a good eye to the job of directing, Mr. Morita and later cinematographer James Gardner helped me with the rest.

1 Brand Manager
2. Agency Producer
3. Account Supervisor
4. Account Executive
5. Director
6. Writer
7. Art Director
8. Cinematographer
9. Assistant Director
10. Grip
11. Gaffer
12. Script & Continuity
13. Talent
14. Properties (Props)

15. Best Boy & worker
16. 1st & 2nd Assistant Camera
17. Sound
18. Boom Operator
19. Set Decorator
20. Carpenter
21. Painter

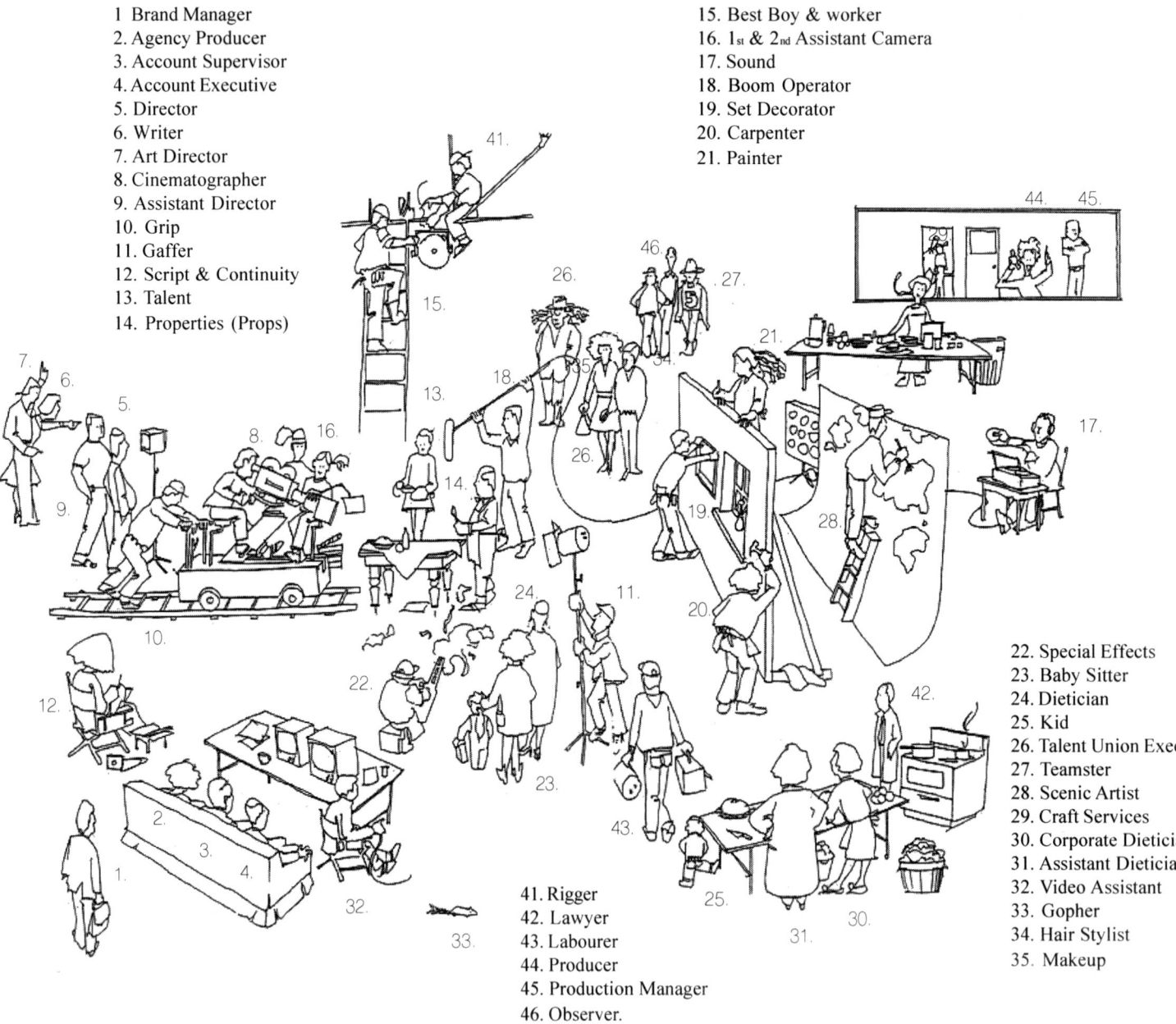

22. Special Effects
23. Baby Sitter
24. Dietician
25. Kid
26. Talent Union Exec.
27. Teamster
28. Scenic Artist
29. Craft Services
30. Corporate Dietician
31. Assistant Dietician
32. Video Assistant
33. Gopher
34. Hair Stylist
35. Makeup

41. Rigger
42. Lawyer
43. Labourer
44. Producer
45. Production Manager
46. Observer.

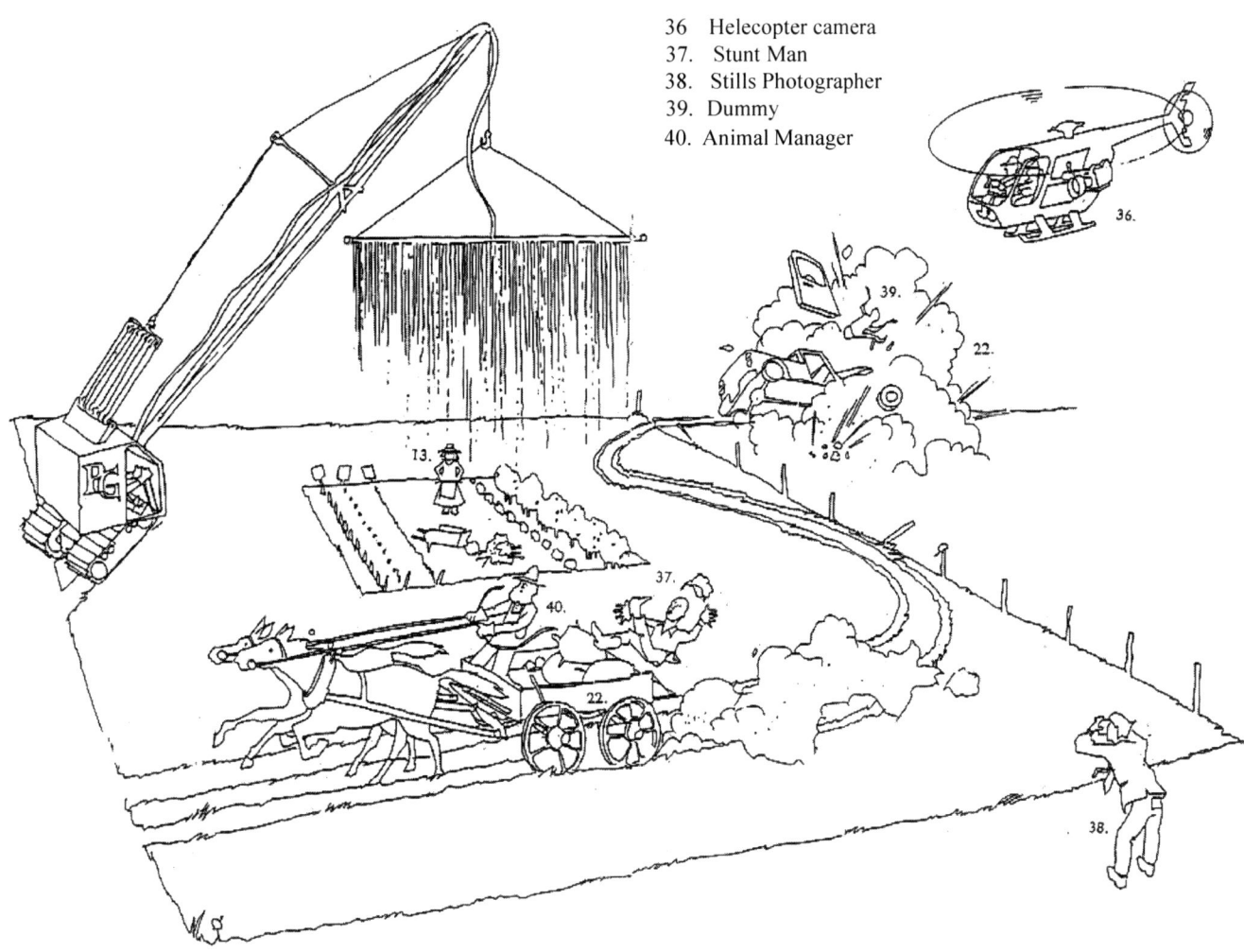

36   Helecopter camera
37.   Stunt Man
38.   Stills Photographer
39.   Dummy
40.   Animal Manager

When a director is on the studio floor, his head is taken up with the flow of the shoot. A crew that works against the director distracts him and lowers the quality of the end product. A disruptive crew member is not included on the next job. In that way, a busy crew, working together, gets to know each other well and trust each other completely. When they are waiting for something like lighting or special effects, they do things to brighten the day. A cinematographer loved puns. An assistant worked with everyone on a story entitled *Jenny and the Brute.* Jenny is short for generator and a Brute is the largest light. The smallest light was an Inky and Inky was in love with an actress named Rolla Velour (a roll of black cloth). The situation is much like a military platoon when everyone takes care of everyone else, humour and good nature grease the wheel.

 I not only had a great cinematographer early in my career but there were other crew members whose skills regularly improved the quality of my work. We had a *grip,* head crew person responsible for safety on the set named "J.D." for John Davidson. Shortly before we began a shoot in the state of Georgia, John was told by a local that poisonous Moccasin snakes made their nests in the lily pad pond we were about to walk into. He sent his assistants flying to collect parts for a stable four-man raft. and had it constructed inside of an hour. While we waited for the raft to be built, a local fellow walked up, threw his bait into the water and pulled out a snapping turtle the size of a dinner platter. He slit its throat, tucked it under his arm, smiled in our direction and said, "Soup for lunch."

A fellow everyone called Whiz Bang was our most consistent
properties person. Whiz Bang was fast, skilled in crafts and owned
a single engine aircraft. His skills helped him win first prize each year for the
airplane's care and attention. His best friend was a brown and white mutt whose
ears and belly dragged on the ground. The last time I asked that he be booked for a
job his agent replied,

"Sorry, Bang and Mutt are in Moose Jaw."

The closest Whiz Bang and I ever came to failure was a shoot in which we were to show a baby's first
step. The way we attempted to catch this infrequent event was to book four babies. Baby #1 had
already taken his first step but was still a little wobbly. Babies #2 & #3 were close to the event and
Baby #4 was approaching but hadn't managed it yet. On the shoot day it was discovered that #2 & #3
had taken their first step the day before. Whiz Bang and I rigged those two babies in diapers with
strings attached so we could hold them back a bit and make them look less skilled. On the shoot day,
#1 was judged to be too expert and #4 not close enough to do the job. When we put them on the set
ready for camera, baby #2 accepted her rear string as new toy intended for play. She would turn,
swing about without loss of balance and play with the string. Baby number 3, given his chance, raced
forward, pulled off both string and diapers and went racing about in his bare bum to escape his mom.
By 4.00 p.m., all the spectators, client and crew, were in a state of despair when someone whispered,
"look!" Number 4, who had been allowed to sit on the rug to watch the events, had a good grip on a
rocking chair. The cameraman panned over, rolled camera and caught our least likely baby pulling
herself erect, releasing the chair and actually taking, arms outstretched, her legitimate very first steps.
Just in time for supper.

An assistant to a *gaffer,* who is a person responsible for lighting, caught my eye on a cosmetics
shoot. The scene included a young and very attractive woman who was wrapped in a towel
shaving her legs. The assistant kept moving black 'flags' that control lighting effects, to places
that could not affect the lighting. When I finally asked him what the hell he was doing, he
whispered, "Taking care of the lady." He had noticed a fellow among the observers who
kept moving to a spot where he could see between the folds of the young woman's towel.
The assistant gaffer became a favourite and a regular member of the crew.

Performers are more relaxed when they understand that everyone around them is working to their
benefit and they are members of the same team.

Q. Was the Tempra commercial scripted?

A. The Tempra commercial shows a series of children explaining how they felt when they had a cold.

The shoot was done with a slightly elevated platform for the kids to sit on. The director lay on a carpet in front of the children and the camera shot over his head. This was done so the children would appear to be speaking to the camera. A one-way mirror, reflective screen, was stretched across the back of the studio to limit distractions for the kids . I was given a list of comments written by the Agency creative department that I gave the children to say. I altered the Agency comments, sometimes feeding them to a child before they expressed their own feelings and sometimes after. We shot a great many kids for two days. The script person's notes gave no indication of the source of the children's lines, either their own or the Agency's and the editor was asked to include the lines he thought were the most interesting. Everyone was amused to find that the final cut included only the children's spontaneous lines. During the casting, an unusual, character-filled little girl came in but decided she was shy. In spite of her mother's best efforts, she would not say a word. Casting is a cooperative process where the director, the writer and the art director do their best to reach an agreement. The team decided to bring the little girl to the shoot in case she would give us a nod or expression. When she saw the set and the other children talking, she walked in, lisped up a storm, both hands waving and full of expression. Four commercials (one 30' and three 10's) were cut from her performance alone.

A similar result took place on a Bell Telephone shoot where children were asked to look amazed when a grandparent opened the front door. There were fake grandparents and real grandparents who had been flown in from all over the country. Every take chosen for the spot was a child reacting to his or her real grandparent.
See Tempra at williamirish.info

Q. Who creates the idea for a commercial?

A. The Agency art director and/or writer.

The process appears to be casual and approximate. It is not. The need for a commercial is first realized inside the company that makes the product. One example comes from General Foods' Maxwell House coffee and at some point in the coffee's life span, someone decided that ground beans made better coffee if they were fresh. Public opinion was gathered by the Research Department and it was confirmed that the public agreed fresh ground coffee beans were a good idea. A process was invented for vacuum packed ground coffee. The factory changed the production lines to suit. An attractive English/French label was outsourced to art studios and the advertising agency was informed that print ads and television commercials were required. To shorten the story, the Agency produced what was needed and the product hit the store shelves in Ontario and Quebec.

A panic ensued in the halls of Imperial Tobacco in Montreal. The American Tobacco company that advertised with popular Marlboro Man commercials was coming to Canada. At least that was the message sent by Imperial's best under-cover spy. The second message gleaned from Imperial's intelligence sources was that a test commercial for the U.S. product was to be put on air in the town of Peterborough, Ontario in two weeks. Two weeks to counter a threatening intrusion. Panic settled with the problem now defined.

A product manager pointed out that American Tobacco had a major difficulty to overcome. Imperial Tobacco had bought the name Marlboro for Canadian usage several years earlier. Marlboro U.S. had to have a name other than Marlboro on the threatening package. Imperial Tobacco called McKim Advertising, McKim called Partners Film Co. and I was told to bring a stills camera and be on an aircraft bound for Calgary the following day. On the flight west, the director was briefed and told that he was to shoot three Canadian Marlboro Man commercials and a stills shot for the new package of Canadian Marlboro cigarettes.

By the time the crew landed in Calgary, it had been decided to shoot images of a cowboy herding fast running horses, a cowboy in the badlands looking for a runaway sheep and a third story that has departed my memory.

Actor cowboys were brought to a casting and it became obvious that only the drop dead handsome went to casting sessions in Calgary and the square and rugged stayed on the ranch. I drove out to Cochrane and found a bar at the bottom of the hill on the edge of the tiny rural town. The perfect cowboy sat in the middle of the room with a lady friend, a beer and a cigarette. My awful opening line, "Hey Mr., how'd ya like to be in films?" gave me the laugh I had hoped for and after a few minutes of conversation, the assurance that I had found the right cowboy. The young man had been a full time cowboy since he was fourteen and had risen to the position of manager of a large herd of Hereford cattle. The story about the shooting of the lost sheep is on page 55.

On completion of the shoot, the footage was rushed to Toronto for processing and a quick edit. The Canadian Marlboro commercials hit the test market in Peterborough the same day as the American Marlboro cigarettes. The cigarettes in the American packages were Marlboro cigarettes labelled Maverick. The cigarettes in the Canadian packages were an Imperial Tobacco brand wrapped in Marlboro papers and a Marlboro package. The public was completely confused and both brands were dead in a week. All of which constituted a nice clean marketing victory for Imperial Tobacco.

Still on the question of who comes up with the idea for an ad, I have seen ads and commercials that manufacturing companies, ad executives, advertising agency creative departments and directors have written and as in the Tempra commercial above, ones where the performing talent wrote their own commercial. The usual process however, is that after the manufacturer has clearly identified what the communication problem is, the advertising agency takes over and produces research to define the consumer they wish to interest. Then the problem is passed along to the *Creative Department.* The so-called *Creatives* who invent and never actually create anything, are the people who most often find interesting answers.

On the sixth rejection by the client of body copy for a newspaper ad to announce a new location for Union Gas, the frustrated ad executive asked if the client would like to write his own words. The client replied, "Good idea!" and wrote out what he wanted, handed them to the executive with the words, "Use these and I don't care what kind of image you put with them." The following is the end result.

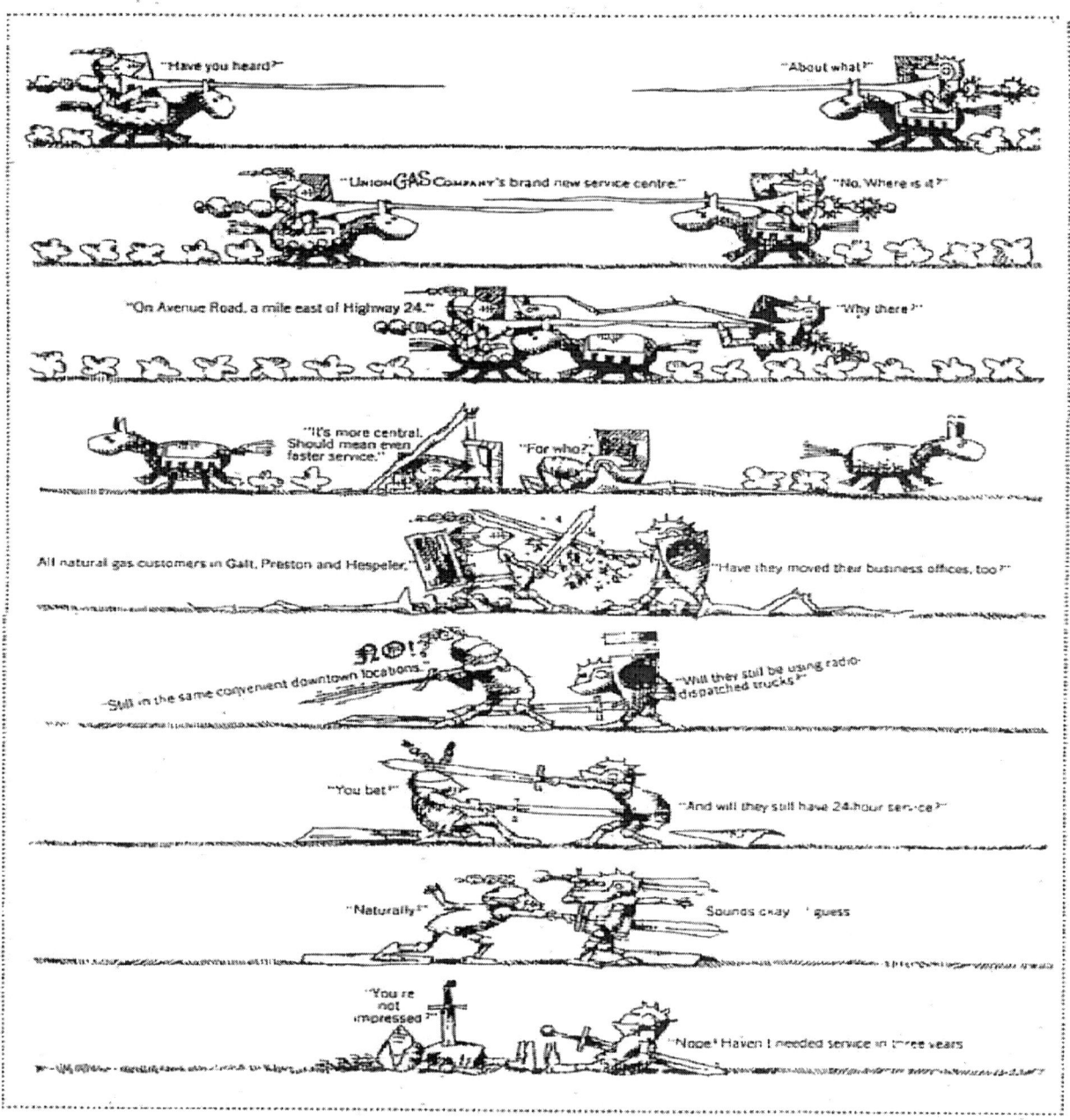

Q. What is the best way to direct talent?

A. Young or old, gorgeous or ugly, more able and less able, treat your performer with respect.

Occasionally almost-famous performers need to convince everyone they are more important and act out to prove this importance. Leslie Nielsen was hired to do a series of Bank of Montreal commercials. On the first shoot, he diminished the very shy sound man. In the Nova Scotia portion of the shoot, the producer learned that it was Mr. Nielsen's birthday. She baked him a cake and made a little party. Mr. Nielsen drank too much and threw the cake at her. On the last portion of the shoot which was to take place in Yellowknife, he asked the producer to fly ahead, greet him when he arrived with a big sign and shouts of "Hello Leslie Nielsen." Mr. Nielsen's brother was an important politician in the North and he wanted to see if he could stir up a big fuss.

I am told Mr. Nielsen, not long after the shoot, modified his impulses. Mr. Nielsen's performances were adequate for the job.

On a shoot for Coca-Cola that featured Bill Cosby, in which I was not involved, Mr. Cosby phoned ahead and explained that he did not have the full half hour he had promised and could everyone please be ready to shoot when he arrived. After a few moments in make-up, he walked onto the set and delivered his lines to camera. The director asked Mr. Cosby to please shave a second or two from his delivery in a second take. Mr. Cosby shaved one and one half seconds from his lines, shook hands with everyone and left. It is a relief to occasionally experience the total professional who barely needs

More often than not, the largest mistake you can make is choosing the wrong talent. Be extremely careful. Children are difficult to read and when they decide to say *no* there is not a thing you can do about it. The system I use to learn if a child will work with me, involves testing their territorial imperative i.e. how secure they feel when a person comes close to them. At a distance of ten feet or more from their parent, I ask the child to come and talk to me. I kneel so that the child's eyes are about the same level as mine. If they answer my questions from that position, look me in the eye and engage in a back and forth conversation, I am assured they will do what I ask of them on the shoot day. If they are too young to talk, it is still informative to find out how afraid they are. Have a back-up. There are three categories of performer who are paid according to their category. The *extra* whose face is not seen is paid the least. The *silent on camera* (S.O.C.) whose face is seen but does not speak, is paid a little more. A performer who is designated *voice on camera* (V.O.C.) receives the largest amount. The kind of performer you do not need is a fellow I hired as an "extra" in a crowd scene. He had a habit of turning his face to camera so he would be an SOC instead of an *extra* and would earn a higher rate. I explained to him that I was aware of what he was doing and asked that in future would he please check on the name of the director before coming to the casting. If it was my shoot, he would not be hired in any category. Another fellow, who liked to play tricks, changed his shirt between scenes so he could claim to have been hired for two jobs. The ACTRA rule book reads, "When the actor's wardrobe is changed, the performer must be paid for two parts."

Q. What process is used for creating an original idea?

A. More often than not, if you worry about an answer, emotion will push an answer into your head. In a situation where you have something NEW to promote, use the word "NEW" because it has the strongest draw on consumers interested in that category of product. How honest you are about your use of the word NEW will set consumer response to your product and company. Let's assume you have a problem and the answer to your problem refuses to visit your brain. The following is a successful system for squeezing solutions from cerebral tangles. Versions of this process were used by Edison, General Nimitz, Singer(sewing machines), Longfellow, Voltair, Arthur Conan Doyle, Eugene O'Neil, Joseph Conrad, Stephen Leacock and a thousand others. I.B.M., Intel, Chrysler, B.F. Goodrich and almost all corporations of note expect their employees to have a standby creative process to use when the answer to a problem doesn't pop up right away.

1. Write out the problem in its shortest form.

Frequently a problem has sub-problems.

Approach them one piece at a time and in order of importance.

2. Estimate how much time you have.

If an answer is needed by morning, you can't spend a week doing research.

3. Gather as much information as you can from as many sources as you can.

The more you learn, the more combinations can be tested by your brain.

4. Answers will pop into your head.

Write everything down - all the ideas your rational mind will give you, even the silly ones.

5. Randomize (go to unrelated subjects) and push the knowledge you have into new areas.

IBM used a spinning device that produced random words.

Turn the pages of magazines on related and unrelated subjects.

6. If you have gathered your information and begged your mind for answers, take a break.

I use the word begged because wanting to succeed increases your chances. Joseph Conrad got his best ideas in the bath. An author of intricate novels got his best ideas in church. Winston Churchill napped. Robert Service and Thoreau walked. Not together. Admiral Nimitz used the pistol range and tennis courts. Brahms shined his shoes. Thomas Edison used new problems to give him relief from the old ones. Charles Darwin rode in his carriage and could always remember the place in the road where the solution to his problem arrived in his head.

7. Go over everything you have written down.

You will have answers from several parts of the process.

Q. Are you a freelance director or do you work out of a production house?

A. I was first hired as a director, by a production house named Rabko. Later seven of us got together to form Partners Film Company. The production house idea was better for me financially because as a partner in a company, I earned two amounts of money, one through a daily rate, the other from the value of shares in the company. When directors work freelance, they are paid by the production house. Their money comes later because the production house is paid first. The advantage to freelance means directors can manage their own time, accepting or rejecting jobs offered to them. When employed in a production house, the director has to support the house and accept all jobs offered. A production house protects and promotes its directors.

Q. Have you had a good idea and then had it stolen?

A. One of my partners phoned me long after I had retired and said, "Just wanted to confess that I have borrowed your *Ontario Milk Board Father and Baby* shot." My response was, "Gee, thanks, I've always liked that one too." I was not concerned that much had been stolen. The fellow was a good director but the cameraman I used was better than his. For our shoot, we had chosen a well muscled gymnast and sat him on the floor in front of, and with his back to his year-old boy. Both sort of stripped to the waist. The baby was framed by his nicely muscled father and as he watched his father, the baby brought his arms up and moved them in perfect imitation of his father. The addition of some skilled lighting and a long lens to square the image, produced an attractive moment.

Q. How do you go about making a commercial?

A. The process begins when the production house receives that illustrates an idea of how to promote a product or solve a problem. The production house asks the director of the Agency's choice, to draw up a *director's treatment* of the board. It is then sent to the Agency, quote attached. The Agency has sent the same request to at least two other production houses and is looking for the best combination of ability and cost.

This is the Agency's storyboard. The problem it was meant to solve was a reduction in popularity for Canadian Tire because of a public squabble amongst the owners.

The production house complies with the Agency's request and sends in return, a Director's Treatment Board and a careful quote. The Agency had does careful testing on the marketing effectiveness of their storyboard. The director does his treatment of their idea, and is careful to limit his changes to the efficiency of the communication and the strength of the visual and emotional qualities of the story. The Canadian Tire story is on page 64 and the

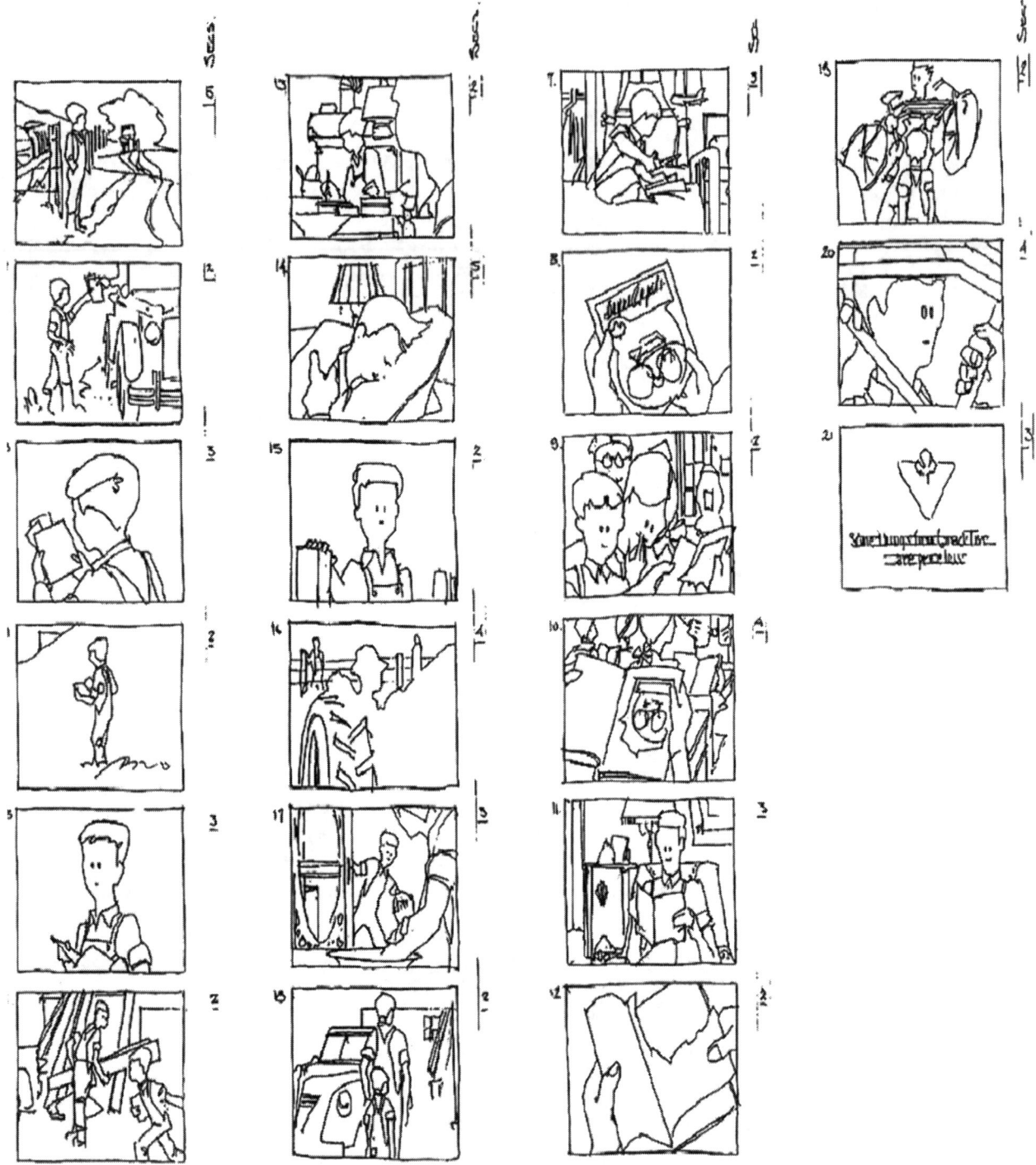

A3. If the treatment and quote are accepted, a production house producer then works with a production manager to decide the how, where and when. They book the cinematographer, gaffer (lighting), grip (boss of the floor), props, sound person, specialists and all the many support people and assistants. Note image on pages 22 and 23. The director specifies the order in which he would like to shoot, draws sets and makes a list of the shots he will shoot.

The *Shot List is given* to everyone
so they know ahead of time exactly
what the director is going to attempt within his time constraints.
Directors who do not use a *Shot List* are slower than those who do.

A4. The *location person* finds an appropriate location for the shoot and the shoot is completed most often on the day it was scheduled because the Agency media department has booked specific times and places for the commercial to be shown.

A5. The footage from the shoot is screened by all and given to the film editor who cuts it together, adding voice over, sound effects, music and the product's identification logo on the end. As actually happened in the example of Canadian Tire, an able editor transformed good footage into a coherent and strong story. The editor's name is Mick Griffin. Because of his edit, the commercial won the Golden Bessie Award at the Canadian Television Bureau awards and was well received by the public.

A6. The editor made copies for the T.V. stations and everyone was paid.

A7. If a shoot runs overtime, a reason is agreed upon and the responsible parties pay the extra. If disaster ensues and the shoot is not completed, or causes damage to someone or something, then the insurance companies kick in. No shoot, ever, is begun without complete and expensive insurance coverage.

Q. How do you decide what to shoot?

A. What the director is going to shoot is decided by what is on the agreed upon treatment storyboard. The *shot list* which is compiled by the director follows the *storyboard* and is the best indicator of how and what the director intends to shoot. The director's contribution comes from what he shoots, how he shoots and how he and the editor make everything knit together. Very occasionally there are jobs when the director is given a subject and told to make a story out of it. An example of that happening was the Honda commercial where they said, "Just show the public how the car is made."

Q. Have you ever done a commercial the client was unhappy with?

A. I am tempted to answer "of course not" but the truth is very different.

Through a late summer's night with a make believe moon and six inches of soap snow, I did my best to shoot a story about a four-year-old boy who saw Rudolph the Red Nosed Reindeer through the side window of his parents' car. I was told it had to be a real reindeer with the red nose added later and the boy must speak clearly when he tells his parents that Rudolph is outside the window. After the real deer had enjoyed his thirty-fifth try at crossing the road in the car's headlights, and he and the humans were slipping on the remnants of the greasy snow, dawn threatened and disaster loomed. It was 4.00 a.m., the boy, fresh from bed, was in the back seat. The key grip was driving, the cameraman was squished on the floor of the back seat pointing a large camera at the little boy. The director was sitting backwards in the front seat attempting to give gentle instructions, when the little boy's face contorted in a look of abject terror. When asked to say his line, he shook his head left and right, left and right, left and right.

The Agency creative director, the Agency producer, the writer and the art director were released from the employ of the advertising agency. On the day the client manufacturer was notified of the disaster, the account was removed from the Agency.

For some unknown reason, the production house, the director and his crew were all paid for their labours. The dumb director had said "yes" to do the dumb project. Story on page 69.

On a studio shoot, an attractive living room set was constructed. A long curved staircase descended into the room and at the base of the stairs an oriental rug held a soft couch. The situation required a small child to descend the stairs in his one piece pyjamas and travel over to his father who was asleep on the couch. He was to throw himself onto his parent who would wake and give him a hug. Take #1 was perfect. Down the stairs, across to daddy and plop for a hug. Father sat up for the hug and as the two came together, father opened his mouth and began to scream. He screamed and screamed until we all rushed over. Blood poured down his chest and his left breast was tightly clamped in the little boy's teeth. Father went to the hospital and the little boy, now quite upset by everyone's response, retired to the dressing room. End of shoot. When I asked the little boy why he had bitten the man, his response was that his mom had told him to do this picture-thing and he didn't want to do it. A new rule. When casting children, show them what they are going to do and always ask them if they would like to do the job.

Q. Is working with children difficult?

A. Children who want to work with you are almost always easy to work

with, but their temperament can change depending on how you treat them. If you are all sweet and sticky, they know they can push you around. If you are straight and respectful and they have a good set of parents, they are marvellous. Children's minds are richly inventive and they just do things that come into their mind. Three, seven-year old girls who were waiting for their turn to be on camera, decided to skip. Two girls swung the rope and a girl in yellow shorts jumped. Every five or six jumps, her shorts slipped far enough that, on the next jump, she would have to yank them up. It was engaging so I shot the little girl in yellow shorts yanking up her pants.

A little boy had to chase a runaway bobsled. He chased the bobsled on cue. but every third step was a leap into the air making a shot of pure enthusiasm.

A little girl, asked in casting how old she was, held up her hand, popped up three fingers one at a time, and replied, "I am pwactising to be fwee."

Two tiny kids, on a ship going up the west coast spotted each other on the observation deck, ran to meet each other, then stood with their noses six inches apart and didn't move or speak for five minutes.

On a plane from Toronto to Vancouver, I was snuggling in for a good rest when an attractive woman crouched down in the isle beside my seat. "Sorry to disturb you. Please, would you come with me?" A little mystified and unused to the attention of mysterious women, I followed the lady back to her seat where she introduced me to a six foot, clean, tidy and handsome young man. We shook hands and the woman said "He's your Bell Telephone boy from the bus and he's on his way to the University of British Columbia."

Q. What is the story behind the Air Canada commercial?

A. That story is covered on page 53 and is worth a read.

Q. How do you inspire talent?

A. Commercial directing is different from feature film directing because the latter has a

preponderance of performers who are heavily experienced professionals. Commercials more often contain performers with a lower level of experience, and some performers with none at all. I enjoy the range of experience in performers because it tests my read of the human and my own ability to help the performer do a good job. The bus driver's response to the Bell Telephone boy from the previous page, was wonderfully accurate. Full story on page 71.

Every performer is different. If you like people, you will be sensitive enough to give them the right incentive. If you don't like people, or are unable to read them, shoot direct-action films with blunt and unsubtle stories. In preparing for a performance, the director outlines why the performer is saying his or her lines. He gives the performer background and where he expects emotion to affect the sequence. One of the most beautiful things to watch is how an actor responds to other persons in the scene, and says what would be natural for him to say in that circumstance. Actors help each other. Build the performer's confidence and if he looks troubled, ask him how you can help. He will ask you good questions in return. There are feature directors that show their performers exactly what they want them to do, to the point of walking through the performance, and showing the performer what and when. I think that removes invention from the actor and the director loses a variance he might have liked better.

In a studio shoot for cosmetics, the capable and mature looking woman was surrounded by sheets of white no-seam paper. The effect bounced light around so there were no shadows, and the woman's skin looked soft and young. The woman had some lines to speak and while she was not a perfect performer, her takes were getting better with each try. Suddenly, she straightened her body, and burst into makeup-mashing-tears. All took a break, knowing we had to reconstruct and I went to the make-up room. I waited for her to calm down and gently asked her why she had broken down. "I can see a woman's face between the sheets of paper, and every time I try my lines, she shakes her head back and forth." We got rid of the substitute director, a spectator, and got an excellent take in three tries.

If you don't know what to do, ask your *cinematographer/cameraman* who will always know what is needed and how the shoot goes together. Another advisor is your script person, but you should have had this worked out either in your head or in a *shot list*, well before the shoot.

Be prepared to tell your client in a pre-production meeting exactly what you are going to do.

Q. Have you ever had a vision but the final result has strayed from that vision?

A. In the hills behind Denver Colorado, there is a place called Steamboat Springs. Our crew
went there with about thirty-five talent and crew to shoot a series of Skidoo commercials. The
locals hired to work in support positions surprised us with their Skidoo abilities and turned out to
be the local mountain rescue team. Somewhere near the middle of the shoot, with only portions of
the commercials completed, our client from Skidoo Corporation in Montreal arrived to see how we
were doing. We took him into the snow covered hills on a Robin Nodwell Tracked Carrier and set
up. Before we rolled, he asked if he could direct the shot. Of course we acquiesced and let him
stand behind the camera and yell orders. While the camera was rolling, a Skidoo messenger with
a telegram, popped over a hill and spoiled all the white stuff we needed in the shot. It turned out
o.k. for a couple of reasons. First, the client was so excited about being a director, he jumped up
and down as he shouted his orders. The jumping caused excessive camera shake, and the shots
he directed were of no use. Secondly, the Skidoo message read, "STOP!!!! NO COMMERCIALS
NEEDED - RESEARCH SAYS MARKET HAS REACHED ITS PEAK. INVENTORY ADEQUATE
FOR THIS SEASON - STOP!!!" So, we all packed up and trundled off home, paid, but no commercials. This story with the dirty details is on page 59. But maybe that isn't quite what you meant.

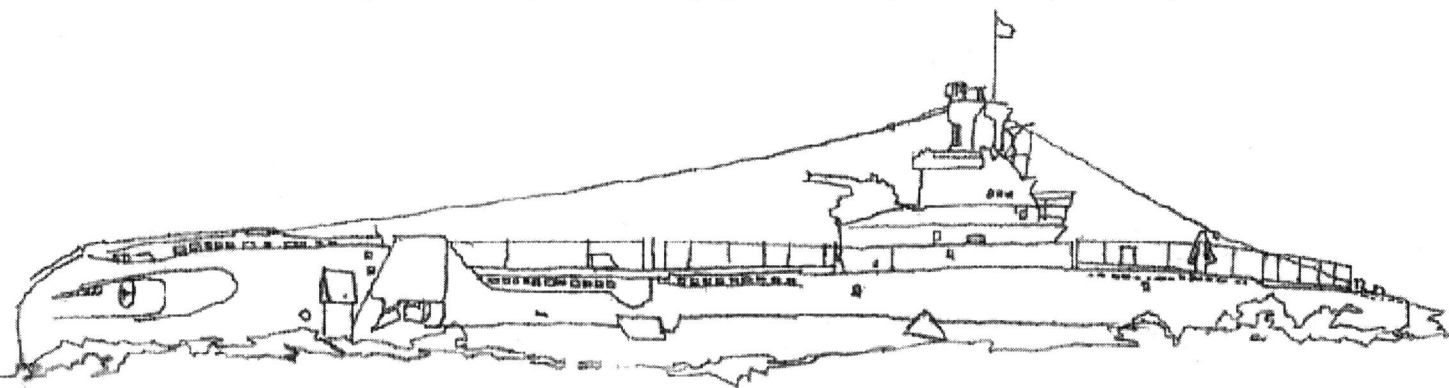

I was brought a commercial about a submarine. The Agency storyboard needed no director
revisions, it read well and would shoot well. I didn't know very much about submarines, so I asked
for and was granted permission to visit one. I drove to Halifax and spent ten minutes with a
gentleman in spotless Navy whites. Lieutenant Agnew was an assistant to the Admiral in charge
of submarines. He took me to a dock and down into a submarine recently purchased from Britain
- one of several cigars packed side by side. Many of the devices inside the sub were covered
with drop cloths because they were secret. By the time I squeaked back up the ladder to the
upper deck, I had a good sense of what a sub felt like. Lt. Agnew took a long time to join me
topside. When his head appeared in the hole in the deck, I was concerned. "Are you o.k. sir?"
He smiled as the rest of him appeared, "Can't get any grease on my whites, got a meeting with
the Admiral." I was treated handsomely by the Navy.
The spot was shown on the air until it was discovered, in tests, viewers had difficulty remembering
the product name. The commercial was yanked and a whispered, "Novahistex" added.
Film at williamirish.info

Few commercials are abandoned because more time is spent inventing, reviewing, testing
rationalizing and explaining them, than is spent shooting them. You enter the shooting
process with everything listed and prepared. If there is a flaw, it is usually discovered before
the shoot. If the shoot goes awry, you shoot it again or adjust it until it is right.

The reverse of disaster happened often. Many commercials turned out better than they were expected to and the most common reason was that someone in the process was willing to make an exceptional contribution. Cinematographer, George Morita, was consistent in making exceptional contributions. View the "Mr. Christie" commercial that won more than its share of attention at williamirish.info. The advertisement contains a series of vignettes, each with different kinds of lighting and a shot of a boy reading a book while he sits on a dock at the lake. Even though water reflections ripple on the boy's feet, there was in reality, no lake at all. Mr. Morita and the properties manager created a completely believable exterior scene in a studio.

A commercial arrived from a company named Motoski. Attached to the commercial was a good looking writer wearing a rumpled green suit and shoes that gave his sockless feet contact with the floor. The script was a good one, simple and clearly presented. The writer wanted us to convince the public that a Motoski was the toughest machine on the market and he wanted us to shoot it near the Motoski factory at La Pocatiere, Quebec. It was a simpler time, well before shoots became heavily crewed. We went to work on it with a producer, a cinematographer and a guy from the factory to drive the machine. The cinematographer was an unusually good looking Dane, very tall and strong. In the process of shooting what I gave him to do, he received a full concussion in a fall into the river, while hanging on the Motoski with one hand and shooting with the other. He received a sprained knee while tied to the front of a chase vehicle, multiple abrasions and a broken right arm. He refused to wear safety belts and in a subsequent shoot, fell out of a chopper door while shooting from a great height. After being completely free of contact with the aircraft, he returned by catching the top rim of the door with his left hand. I believe at the time there wasn't another cinematographer who could have given of himself the way this man did.

The commercial won the Gold Bessie in the TV Bureau Awards of 1975.

More details on page 51.

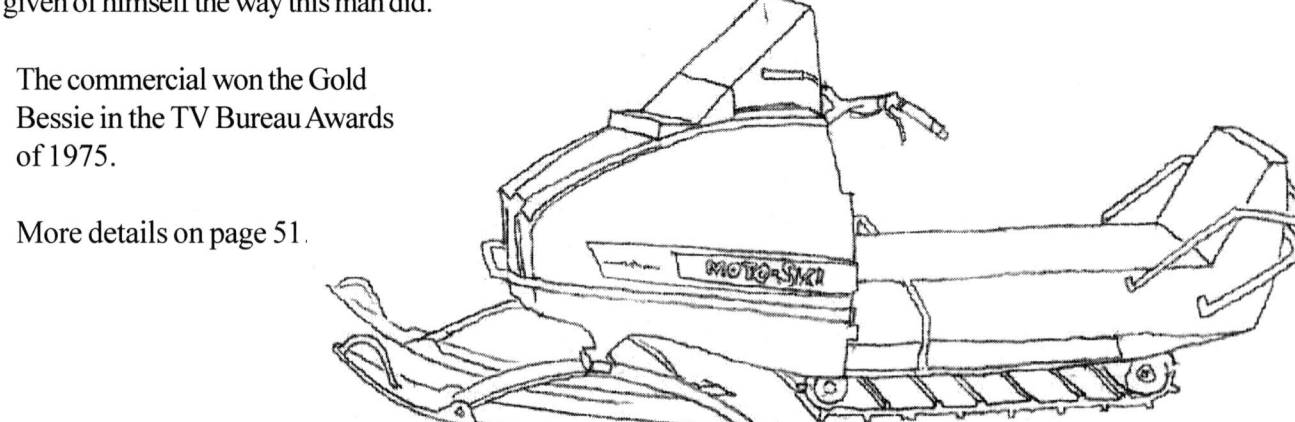

Q. What insight can you give me about working in the industry?

A. Commercial film is an appendage of the marketing industry. There are many interesting jobs in marketing. Advertising agencies require research people, media people, account executives, writers, art directors, management and financial people. All of those catagories give good remuneration and challenging projects. A good company will enhance your knowledge with a mix of interesting courses. If your question is relevant only to film direction, the process of finding your way is the same as a good boxer winning a place in his industry. Neither one of these occupations require a university degree. A degree does provide benefits, your reel is much more important. Writers, art directors, artists, photographers, cinematographers and directors can have zero accreditation, wear gum boots and have holes in their shoes and be hired in a flash if their reel shows ability. A senior creative director, owner of occasional advertising agencies, was hired out of a restaurant kitchen where he washed dishes because someone read his book of poetry. If work in a marketing job is what you would like to try, take a course. If writing, art or directing interests you, make a reel or a sample book. Start now. Sweep studios for free.

The young lady's name was Catlin and she had wormed her way into film production with the influence of her father. On her first day at the production house, she wore jeans and a pink 'T' shirt. The next day, every single male in the production house wore jeans and a pink 'T' shirt. Joseph had to soak a white shirt for an hour with his red long johns before he got the right shade of pink. Catlin took it all in good humour; she was bright and became a good worker and friend to all. When she had watched numerous productions and worked in several positions, she left the production house and got a job in an advertising agency as a junior art director. Her abilities progressed and she turned up one day back at the production house as a full blown Agency art director with a job she wanted us to shoot. I got the job as director and joined Catlin and my cameraman and just a few others, on a tour of the Honda factory. I did wonder at the effect of a beautiful woman in a male dominated factory. What happened, impressed me and gave me a permanent memory with smile attached. No, they didn't pull out their pink 'T' shirts, they were very gentle. As our line of Agency and production people walked from one point of interest to the next, the first worker, who spotted our beautiful young woman, began to whistle quietly. The whistling alerted the next worker in the line, who would clear his throat to alert the next who would sing etc etc. All of them smiled and enjoyed the moment. Catlin was not aware of what took place. The production contingent smiled.

If you want to direct, do not take a crew job because you see it as a form of film work. It's a trap. You end up liking the salary, accepting the next job and the next and you do not have a reel to show for it. Actually I do not have to warn you about this possible fate. The last time I checked, there were fourteen applicants for every job category.

Q. When your crew becomes unmotivated how do you remotivate them?

A. I have never had to re-motivate anyone. If you
use a union crew, we always did, the men and women
are motivated by the rules and a salary scale designated
by their job category. They have too much to lose to
mess up. It they do misbehave, members of their own
union straighten them out. If I did have to straighten
them out, I simply didn't ask for them on the next job.
If you are working non-union, you have to see to the
troublemaker's motivations. A *properties* man thought
I used too much film and loved to make quiet criticisms.
It disrupted my thoughts while I was trying to keep
everything straight. I simply booked another *prop* man on future jobs.

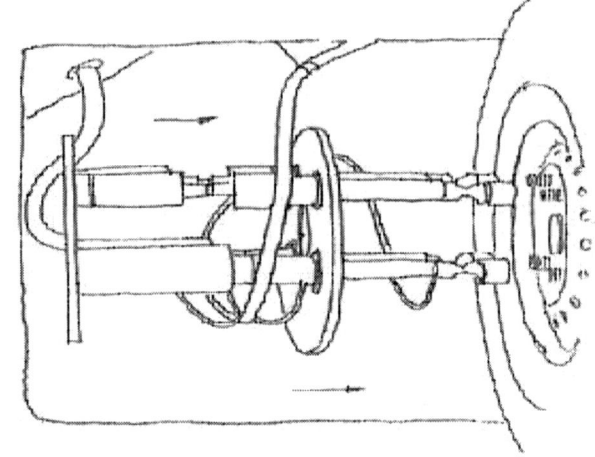

Unions ensure safety, reasonable
pay and a community of
cooperative skilled workers.
I learned to appreciate
ACTRA and IATSI for
keeping a steady flow of
performers and able crew.

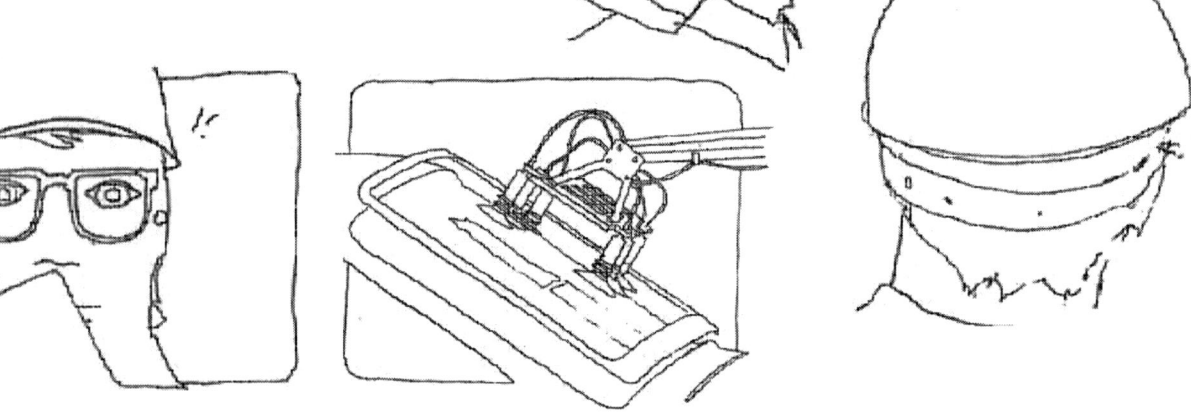

Q. Do you get to pick your own crew?

A. As time goes on, your producer and production manager
get to know who you like to use. It is the case however,
that the cinematographer has a preference for the
composition of *his* crew. This covers a preponderance of
the people hired. Directors gets to choose a smaller
number of workers whose jobs are directly connected to
him, such as props, special effects, stunt person, script
person, and even the cinematographer. A wise director
listens to the advice of all of the members of his crew
and accesses the variety of knowledge that exists on
his shooting floor.

Q. Do you have a choice of the commercials you do?

A. I chose to do everything that came my way because it gave me a broad range of experience.

In forty years of directing, I have refused only three jobs because I disliked what I thought to be a dishonest client or message. I used a personal rating system. If I estimated the value of a concept to be a '4', I would try to raise its value to a '6' or '7'. One day, I was sent a concept by Heinz Ketchup which I rated about a '3'. The director's treatment I sent back to the Agency was as follows. It had nothing at all to do with the concept they sent me. They did not accept it.

1.

2. & 3.

A dinner shoots out of the wall
and is delivered to the dining room.
Pop singer enters, sits and opens the platter
to find no Heinz on his hamburger.
He yells,
and the waiter
bursts into the hall with the Ketchup,
races to the table on a moped
and delivers the Heinz.

4.

5.

6.

7.

8.

Q. Have you worked in countries other than Canada?

A. I have not worked for a production house that was not Canadian. The Canadian production units sent me to Russia, Yugoslavia, France, England, Germany, Scotland, Ireland, Holland, The United States (including Hawaii), Mexico, and every province and territory of Canada except the Yukon. Shortly after I retired, the first of five times, I whizzed off to the Yukon, via the B.C. Coast, Skagway, Whitehorse and Dawson. I rented a car and went up the Dempster Highway, the only road in North America above the Arctic Circle. Why would anyone want to work anywhere other than Canada? The Yukon Territory is larger than the combined size of Great Britain, France and Spain and has only 150,000 residents.

The variety of places I have travelled sounds impressive but in reality it is not. When you are working, you are expected to complete your shooting in a minimum amount of time. Sightseeing is limited to what you can catch as you do a fast location hunt. On a job for Mastercard, we had to land in a country, check into a hotel, have a bite to eat, and split everyone up for individual jobs. The producer arranged a casting, the production manager went in search of vehicles and gear, the director and the cinematographer looked for locations, occasionally in the dark. The sequence was shot in the morning and we caught a plane to the next location in the afternoon. A precis of the shoot is in blog *Miss Adventure* on page 85.

Q. What was your worst directing experience?

A. The day I had to shoot a game arcade for Molson Beer. At a critical and complex moment,

my mind did a cut back to my twenties where, when threatened by difficulties, a black wall would fill my mind and I was rendered mute. Once more, my crew helped to save the day. Or perhaps the worst was the dark night I had to deal with Rudolph? Six of one...

Q. Have you met a lot of famous people?

A. As a junior R.C.M.P. constable, I was asked to stand guard at the Governor General's train

in Ottawa. I walked up and down the boardwalk outside the train, catching the occasional glimpse of the vulture-like stance of Vincent Massey, until a blindingly handsome man in the military uniform of aide-de-camp stepped down from the train. I snapped a perfect salute, I was good at salutes, and then remembered underlings were not supposed to salute an officer who was not wearing a hat because they could not return the salute without a hat. 'Handsome' generously ignored my goof and informed me that Prime Minister Diefenbaker would be arriving in his black Buick, momentarily. My job, he said, was to step forward, open his door, step back and salute smartly. I did a mile or two back and forth on the boardwalk before the shiny Buick pulled up. I stepped smartly forward, opened the rear door for the Prime Minister, stepped back, threw my best salute and the Prime Minister opened his own front door and got out. He was good enough to say, "Thank you son." I was eager to show him I was paying attention and when he exited the train, I again stepped smartly forward, snapped a winner of a salute and opened the front door. Dief opened the back door and got in himself. Dief was the only person whose *fame* I recognized.

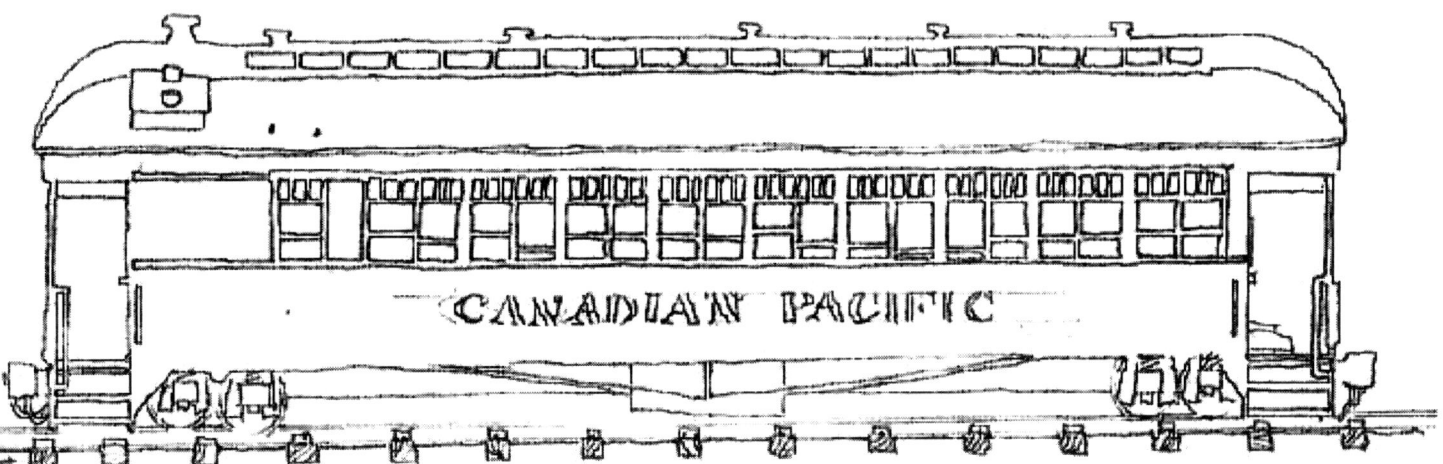

I am not an advocate of the *star* system. In my opinion, good performers should be admired for their abilities. They should not be admired and slobbered over to a greater degree than a good surgeon, a master craftsperson or even a Prime Minister.

Perhaps my attitude is a contributing factor in my experiences with *stars* like Lorne Green and Leslie Nielsen. Martin Short, by contrast, was a charmer. I loved Gilda Radner. She and Andrea Martin would come to casting sessions and leave us heaving with laughter.

Q. Do you ever create your own scripts?

A. No, because I am not party to the marketing knowledge that comes with the script. My
inventions would produce a bent spear for a communication. The only advertising agency
that would ever accept a script, written by someone not on their staff, was Bonneville
Advertising in Salt Lake City. Their only client was the Church of Jesus Christ of Latter Day
Saints and it didn't diminish their abilities to win new clients if it became public that they
had used an outside source. Advertising agencies do not use an outside source. They
advertise their own employees as the best and could never admit to outsourcing. If you
think you would make a good commercial writer, rewrite every commercial you do not like and
submit it to an Agency creative director for comment. A script has to have knowledge of the
product, knowledge of the desired consumer and where the commercial will be shown. As an
outsider, you cannot have knowledge of those facts.

Q. Do ideas change between the office and the shoot?

A. Never on a professional shoot because everything has been pre-tested, questioned, shaved,
researched and meticulously planned. Look closely at the Agency's storyboard on page 27
and compare the shots in the director's treatment on page 28. You will see that the director's
changes do not change the message but add more emotion to the story. Now look at the
finished commercial at williamirish.info. You will see very little variance between the director's
board and the finished product. If the director sees a flaw in the story, he has to make the
changes before the shoot or else he is stuck with them. The director has too many things to
do after his treatment has been approved.

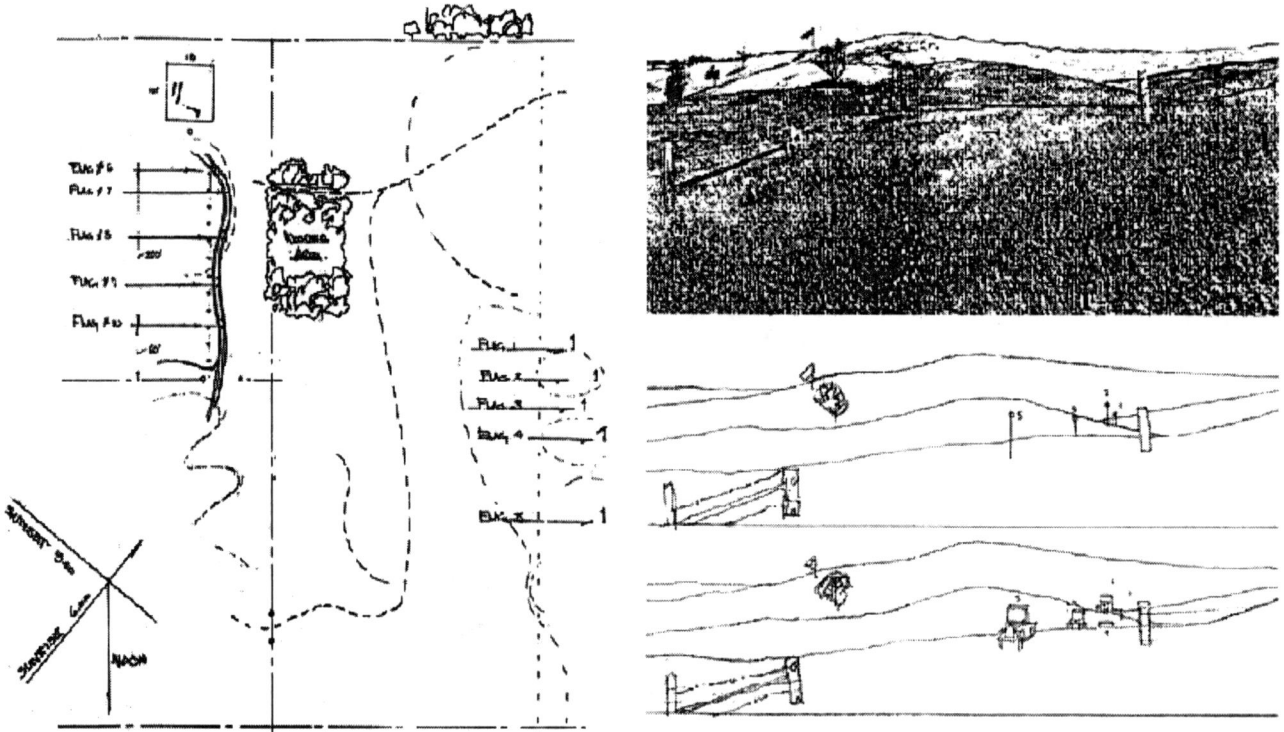

Maps for the Canadian Tire *Bike Story* to inform the crew on how the job was to be shot.

Q. What is done on a field survey?

A. If you mean a survey of the shoot area, all the heads of departments affected by the location, go out to look at the location. The producer makes sure that permissions are intact. The production manager looks to see what he needs to get his trucks in place and the director and cameraman go through the places where the scenes will be shot so they know what to bring to the shoot. The film production house producer ensures the talent will be fed and given a good place to sleep.

In the case of Canadian Tire, the drawings on page 44 were given to each person on the field survey. I had placed stakes in the ground so the cinematographer could stand where I thought his camera should be and discuss the potential of each shot. A wagon road had to be cut out of the grass and a fence added so these additions were marked with flags.

I had assumed that a well-to-do company would have a big budget and I could pick a location somewhere in Saskatchewan. That was not to be and knowing there are not a lot of places in Ontario that look like the prairies, I drove around trying to find a corner that did. On a country road west of Uxbridge, I spotted a hill on the south side of the road that had a prairie like appearance. I knocked on the farm door and made a case for using the hill for a film shoot, to a broad old fellow with a big moustache. When I paused for breath, he leapt in, and in an imperious tone explained that he was Baron such and such from Bavaria and nobody ever came on his land.

Then he slammed the door.

I was disheartened because it was the only place I had found in three days of searching. I turned back and took a side road south remembering that I was at the height of land between Lake Simcoe and Lake Ontario. Driving beside the Baron's farm, it came to me that if I booked the Baron's neighbour's farm, I could use the Baron's hill as background without asking for his permission. The Baron's neighbour was an attractive woman, so I sent my most handsome production manager to ask for permission. Permission was given and the attractive woman made four thousand dollars, the blustering Baron, zip.

Q. How much control does the director have over choosing talent?

A. The director has strong influence on talent selection and Agencies have reasons with which to change his mind. "We haven't got enough money to search further." or "The creatives disagree." In my experience, several good scripts have been ruined with those excuses.

Q. Have you ever made a commercial for a product you didn't like?

A. Many times. The fact that I didn't like the product was irrelevant. If the question means
did I ever accept a job that was morally distasteful to me, the answer is no because in all my
years, that problem did not occur. The opposite occasionally takes place where the idea and
the board are so perfect that no changes need to be made and a director's treatment is not
necessary. This Novahistex story-board from the Agency, was such an occasion.

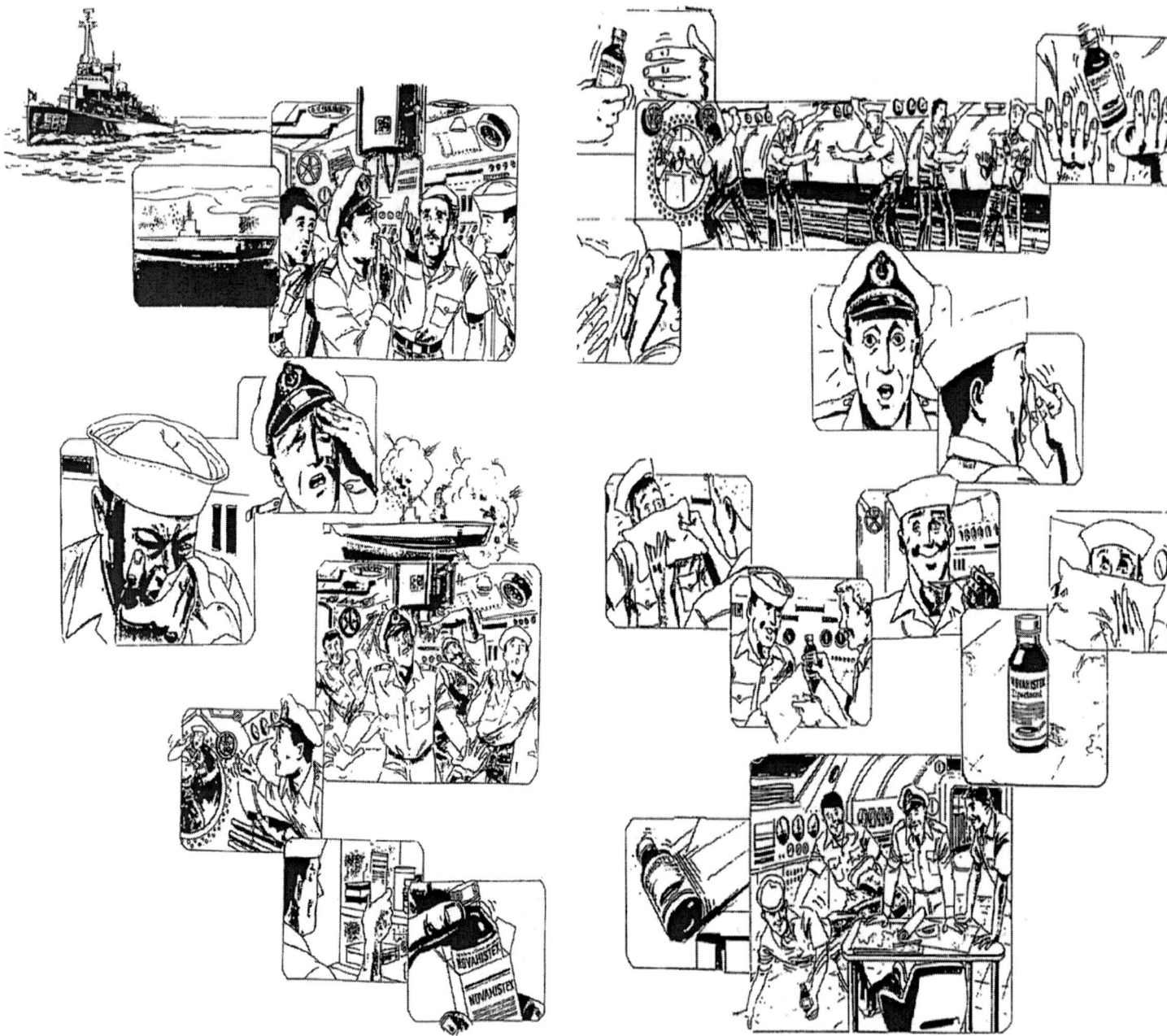

A more complete story is on page 70 and the commercial can be seen at williamirish.info.

Q. Did you have any training as a director?

A. None.
You can learn the technical side of directing
in an afternoon.

It is not a difficult thing to learn to do.
Eventually, just by doing the job, I learned how to
do the technical side. The other part of the
director's job is visual and emotional. Each of us
has his own way of accomplishing that. I had
brought visual and emotional skills with me and
had only the technical side to learn.

Start now.

Build the foundation of mistakes we all need
to support us.

Fear is the engine of invention.

I was discouraged one day and flopped down
on the lobby couch at Rabko Productions. I was deep in
thought when a senior director dropped down beside me. "Bill," he said,
"You're just taking it all too seriously. All you're dealing with is taste." It was a wonderful and
timely piece of information. I missed his advice when he returned home to Speedy Creek.

Q.

Has there ever been a simultaneous video recording of one of your shoots.

A.

By 1980, all professional cameras had a mirror in them that split the image - one half
going to the film side and the other half going to a video side. This feature brought huge
advantages and few disadvantages. Before the addition of the video, the director, the
cameraman and everyone else on the shoot, had to wait until the film was processed and
printed, before they knew exactly what their shots looked like. With the new cameras, the
director and whoever else feels the need, can now watch the video and tell exactly what was
shot, how it was framed, how the product looks, what the colour is and what they have to
shoot next. The difficulty with the new sytem makes for a lot of contention about each of
those subjects. The shoot can be delayed by variations of opinion and interest.

Directors do their best and most efficient work when they are left alone. That situation is a
very rare occasion.

Q. What was your favourite commercial?

A. The tension involved in a commercial shoot pretty much erases enjoyment. Because my focus and experience in advertising agencies included a high interest in achieving the communication objectives, there are several commercials that pleased me because they delivered the message well.

My favourites are Canadian Tire, Motoski, Novahistex, Tempra and Marlboro. The commercials can be viewed at williamirish.info.

We shot an Esso commercial on the old Banff Highway, west of Calgary, that was both a pleasure to do and a pleasure to watch later. While completing another shoot, we had been contacted and asked to shoot the spot for Esso before we came home. Esso wanted to remind their customers that some of their stations had well-qualified mechanics to fix car problems. They thought if we did this and this, this and that, we would give them what they needed. We picked a place with a dip in a two-lane road with a curve that preceded the dip, and set up the shot for sunset. I was in one of my favourite places in the world, only three or four of us, zero pressure and the first B.C. cherries of the year for sale at the roadside. The camera rolled, a car came around the bend and just before it entered the dip, it jerked and began to rattle. It disappeared into the dip and viewers heard the out-of-sight vehicle sputter, click and clank to a stop on the gravel edge. They heard the car door open and slam shut, then muttering, and the sound of footsteps coming up the road. The driver's head slowly appeared over the brow of the dip and his body lengthened as the voice-over reminded the consumer to have their cars checked at Esso. A little more of this story on page 72.

...and we got paid for two jobs.

In 2010-ish, a production company named Rogue Artists
asked me to write a blog a week to amuse
those who accessed Rogue's web site.

Since directors are storytellers, the blogs are
personal histories of film productions.

Productions & Executions

Table of Contents

page 50. Always Pray Before Shooting
page 51. Life is Tough
page 52. Hey Otis, Ya Wanna be in Films?
page 53. Flyin High with lyin' Brian
page 55. Canada's Last Cigarette Commercial
page 57. The Good, Bad and the Ugly.
page 59. A Fine and Productive Failure.
page 60. Animal Tendencies
page 61. Memories
page 62. Disasters Unlimited
page 63. Glutinous Fruition
page 64. Caring
page 65. A Crew For All Seasons
page 67. Wonderkids
page 69. The Terminator
page 70. Sometimes
page 71. Rings a Bell
page 72. S.O.A. & S.O.B.
page 73. Tak
page 75. A Few Degrees from Perfect
page 77. Conversations
page 78. Fake Lakes
page 79. Before the Execution
page 81. Adventure Tours

page 83. Bottoms Up
page 84. Miss Demeanour
page 85. Miss Adventure
page 86. Miss Takes
page 87. Miss Direction
page 89. Short Ends & Leftovers
page 91. Great Expectations
page 92. If.........
page 94. Difference & Dissention
page 95. Greeks & Gifts
page 97. What's Yer Beef
page 98. Exit Stages
page 99. A Saintly Sequence
page 101. Getting it Right
page 102. Mrs. & Misses
page 103. Shooting Blind
page 104. Russia - Part One
page 105. Russia - Part Two
page 107. Russia - Part three
page 108. Russia - Part Four
page 109. Russia - Part Five
page 110. Russia - Last Part
page 111. Authors comment

Productions &Executions

Always pray before shooting

The producer was a fit looking thirty-five-year old. His past contained the dubious accreditations of drug dealer and thief. He bragged on his two gunshot scars and everywhere he went, he carried a powerful telephone system in a sack at his side.

The rental van plucked a large man from a North Vancouver street at 5.30 a.m. It crossed Lion's Gate and proceeded through the streets and avenues of Vancouver proper. A tall slim fellow, from a home near U.B.C., came aboard and sat up front with the driver. The next addition lived in a rooming house and the one after that in a house without lights and no one to wave goodbye. Two hotels produced two more men. The van picked up the director about 6.30 a.m. He was second last on the list. The last was the producer who was allowed more sleep because he was the client, the decision maker and the man with the money.

Rain had begun in the early light. On the way out past Simon Fraser, it thundered down and bounced back up from the road to slow our pace. It softened as we grabbed the Trans Canada and headed for Abbotsford.

Tires whispered and sung and the big man slept. The producer talked to Salt Lake City, Toronto and two other places. Men spoke quietly one to one. When talk slowed, the director outlined the job (a commercial film for the Mormon Church) for the men. He then turned to the producer and asked him to tell the crew what the Church of the Latter Day Saints stood for. The producer showed his usual pleasure at the request and explained the L.D.S. or Mormon Church was a spiritual community that believed Jesus Christ was the Son of God. For them, Jesus provided the path to eternal life. The Community was called Latter Day Saints because they believed the leaders of recent history could add to their body of spiritual understanding.

A small pause and one of the men turned to the big fellow in the back corner and asked, "So, John, what's your religion?" John, dozy and hoping to be funny, grunted "T.V." and rolled his body to the window. The tall fellow in front recognized this exchange might constitute an affront and said quietly, "I am a Jew." After a pause he continued. "We are strong community supporters, both of our own religious community and of the broader community we live in. We believe the God of Israel gave us our credentials. Our ethical foundation comes to us via Moses and our holidays and festivals are commemorations of events like a second century revolt and a war with the Roman Empire."

This quiet and articulate explanation was absorbed. Then the tidy man from the rooming house said, "I am a Muslim. Our religious community is based on obedience to the teachings in the Koran. We have daily regimens that in Canada are usually messed up by our work requirements. Canadian Muslims tend to be more casual than the Middle Eastern ones. We believe the prophet Mohammed spoke for God, and his teachings give us everyday guidance."

A long silence ensued off the ends of the smiles. The vehicle hummed. The sun pushed through. The rich odor of wet cedar filled the van.

Closer to Abbotsford, one of the crew said, "I am a Roman Catholic. The actions of some of the clergy have not supported the pride I have in my beliefs. Human weakness aside, I believe the Pope in Rome to be a primary spiritual authority. It's a convenient religion. I can misbehave on almost any level, go to confession and get back in the lineup for heaven."

A stop at Abbotsford for egg McMuffins and then everyone spread out along a set of railway tracks to start their day. When the sun lowered and warmed the mountain backdrop, they agreed they had managed a productive day and piled back into the van. They picked up the opposite side of the Trans Canada and settled in for the return trip.

The driver spoke as soon as he reached speed. "I want to inform you that I am a First Nations person and the spiritual belief of my people is that God is the tree and the bear and me and the highway."

Productions & Executions

Life is Tough

The different young man, in the green suit and shoes with holes in the soles, worked for McKim, Montreal. He designed concepts and executions for advertisers and although his personal presentation was different, I liked him. His head was clear, clean and right on point. It was 1970ish and our production house was eager to show its worth. When the man from Montreal arrived for a quote, we kept the price thin and showed we were eager to do the job. The job was for Motoski SkiDoo in La Pocatiere, Quebec. The production price the producer was allowed for the job was more than skinny and included only a director, cameraman and a producer. Even the Agency and the Client couldn't afford to come to the shoot.

The cameraman was a tall, handsome Dane-Canadian. He was so handsome women walked up to him on the street and suggested immediate intimacies or marriage. His tendency to accept the former often conflicted with his shooting schedule. He arrived at the shoot in La Pocatiere (north of Quebec City and not on my map) with a leggy Toronto actress.

The guide concept for the commercial was that Motoski Skidoos were tested in the summer to make sure they stood up to rough treatment in the winter. The closing title on the spot was "Tougher Seven Ways." The director and the producer tied the cameraman to the grill of a rental truck and the truck chased the skidoo through untended fields. Not enough money for a rig-building grip, so the cameraman wrapped an arm around the skidoo driver, attached the camera to his head with a bungee cord and tore off up the boulder strewn creek. On the beach, the film cover fell off the camera and was quickly slammed back into place. The side flash on all the beach film looked like a special effect applied at edit. The intentional effect of sparks flashing from the skis was achieved by the cameraman lying across the lap of the driver on a gravel road. The work proceeded for three days; a sandhill jump, a shot of the plant, a long-lens pan through a maple forest .

The shoot went reasonably well. The director enjoyed the freedom of not having the drag of Agency coaching. "Gee, almost like a real director." The difficulty of getting the cameraman out of his tent in the morning slowed things a bit, but a certain amount of consideration was appropriate for the wounds the cameraman had collected.   A bump when he was tied to the truck grill, put some scrapes on a knee. The skidoo in the creek hit a rock, the camera stretched out on the bungie cord that was around his head and delivered a hit that put him out cold and sinking in the creek. On the day of departure from La Pocatiere, he reached down for his suitcase and his arm broke at the elbow. A later assessment showed the difficulty to have come from the overly stressed and stretched muscles that held onto the skidoo driver while he leaned out to shoot the progress of the vehicle through the rocky creek.

The commercial won the top award in the Bessies that year.

The director took the award home and hid it behind a cabinet. When asked why he didn't hang awards on his wall he replied that he had learned from past experience that when awards are hung on the wall, they "talked." The first one sat proudly on the wall for a time but soon began to say, "Well?" Feeling guilty, the director rushed to try for another. When he had five awards, the display greeted him as he walked into the room. "Is this the best you can do?"

He stopped hanging awards on his wall.

The popular commercial had another effect. Bombardier, the company that invented skidoos was threatened by the little La Pocatiere industry and paid well to eliminate the competition by buying them into the Bombardier organization. The cameraman continued to take personal and professional risks. Scuttlebutt has it that on a helicopter shoot, he refused to wear a safety harness. The helicopter hit turbulence and the cameraman found himself free of the aircraft. He stretched his overstretched arm back to the chopper and just managed to catch the door-rim to pull himself back inside.

Productions & Executions

Hey Otis, Ya wanna be in films?

I was gopher-labourer in tiny Wilder film studios on Berkeley Street, Toronto when a Tourism job came in. The regular camera assistant was busy so I was told to learn how to pull focus, "Oh, yes and while you're at it, get on a plane to Nova Scotia, go location hunting and find a performer or two." Life was good.

The Lunenburg docks were recommended for our attention so I found my way there, stood on the docks for a day watching the activity and looking for the perfect Nova Scotia fisherman. On day two, a battered old scallop dragger with iron-clad sides tied up and half a dozen rough looking characters rumbled down the ramp. One of them was wide and strong with a heavy growth and clothes that proved he worked hard for a living. Gathering up my courage, I approached him and asked him if he would help. It was an easy and pleasant affirmation. He told me his name was Otis Hysler and "Yes" he would meet me here at sunrise one week from that day. Half an hour after sunrise, on the alloted day, there weren't any picturesque fisherman on the docks, just the cameraman and I walking impatiently up and down. I wished I had asked for a phone number and finally approached a business man in a beautiful suit to ask if he might know Otis. The business man was of course Otis, all spiffed up and shaved for his film debut. He promised to return to his fisherman appearance in a week. He did, the cameraman shot and I pulled focus. Otis was great.

Otis was a descendant of survivors from a ship that went aground off the coast of Nova Scotia. The survivors were of Dutch heritage and they had intended to become farmers. They came ashore to find not much in the way of farmland, instead a perfect and picturesque harbour tucked into the coast. A resilient people, they became fishermen and boat builders and helped build the modern community of Lunenburg, N.S. The shipwrights became internationally known for their abilities.

They built a ship called the Bluenose then a large ship built in meticulous detail for a film entitled *Mutiny on the Bounty.*

Otis was well known in his community. He lived in a small white house on the hill above town. The pretty house was old but Otis maintained it well. It was very clean. The walks and flowerbeds were lined in carefully placed red, white and blue stones. Inside, everything was dust free and in its place. In contrast to his house, Otis was very rough and rumpled. To give him his due, the roughness was brought about by the way he made his living. He was a seaman who worked on any ship that would take him, for whatever job was available. He stood at average height with a battered black beret smashed on his head. His face was sun-darkened under a crust of snow-white stubble, two bright steady eyes framed in leather, a thick neck and barrel chest. The anatomy of ocean fishermen is sometimes changed by the demands of their work. A man who pulls nets into a dory for half his life has backward hands. The little fingers become as large as the thumbs because the little finger is used to hook the net for second pulls. The demands of Otis's work had created exceptionally large forearms and a grip of iron.

Mr. Hysler enjoyed his life. One day in the year was his favorite. Because the American fishery on the east coast was very similar to the Canadian fishery, there was a lively competition over who was the best at a wide range of fishing skills. On a day agreed to by all, strong men from Halifax and down the coast, came to Lunenburg, as did the strong men from Boston on up. They joined in a vigorous contest of skill and strength. Otis's specialty was the dory race. At the prescribed time, men lined up in schooner dories and at the sound of a gun, were off, pulling for all they were worth. Young men who had trained all year for this moment, did their very best and crossed the finish line exhausted and splayed across their oars. Otis, who was usually the oldest, always won. To add insult to injury, he would cross the finish line grasping the handles of his two twelve-foot-oaken-oars and turn them up vertically, with only the power of his wrists. Each year Otis added a new trophy to the spotless wall of trophies in the little white house on the hill.

Productions &Executions

Flyin' High with Lyin' Brian

They were in a big hurry because the -*whisper whisper* - client wanted to zip this one through. *Whisper, whisper* – government – *whisper* – now damit... so we all rushed into a room, locked the door and were introduced to the project by the agency producer. The Prime Minister had realized that the public was tired of paying the budget overruns of the government-run airline and had decided in a moment of genius to sell Air Canada to the Canadian public. The Canadian public was not yet aware of his intentions ergo -*whisper whisper*-and the law said it was not legal to advertise or sell shares before the privatization had taken place. The Prime Minister however, figured he could load the dice a bit and suggested a commercial that would make the shares more attractive and have the title *Share our Tomorrows* an implied request to purchase Air Canada shares.

The communication concept was that a group of passengers would get on a 1940's DC-3 aircraft, enjoy a pleasant flight and land magically in a supersonic vehicle in the year 2050. We all went to work for the PM with great enthusiasm.

Air Canada had revamped a DC-3 with the latest flying aids and comfortable seats for the transport of not-in-a-hurry executives. The director flew to Calgary where the film crew had commandeered the DC-3. The first location search was for an airport that was visually similar to a 1945-1950 airport. Claresholm, south of Calgary, had a good one with three runways in a triangular formation so it was easier to find a wind direction to lift a DC-3. The designated pilot refused Claresholm. It was apparently twenty feet too high in altitude and a DC-3 needed twelve more feet of runway. The search continued. A rambling location manager called to say that Swift Current, Saskatchewan, aka Speedy Creek, looked good. By this time, someone with knowledge and power over pilots got rid of the fellow who needed twelve more feet and gave us Mister Cool, a 747 pilot in from Bangkok.

Our head grip fixed the aging hangar doors so we could store the old DC-3 overnight. At three in the morning, we gathered to set up the shot for the early morning loading of passengers. They were all there, the sun rose, passengers in costume climbed aboard, the sun flared perfectly in the lens and we had our principal moment. After an interior shot, we covered a glimpse of the handsome man waving in the window and the complimentary shot of his wife, holding a toy doll wrapped in the motel owner's antique table cloth, with an answering wave. It was a tense moment when the new pilot was asked to lift the DC-3 off the runway. He laughed and lifted it off easily inside one hundred feet.

In the early days of air travel, a DC-3 could not achieve enough altitude to fly over the Rockies, and it had to travel through the valleys rather than over the mountains. In deciding how to do a follow shot through the Bow Valley (Banff), we learned that helicopters can not fly fast enough to fly with the DC-3 even when the DC-3 was at its slowest speed. We hunted up a plane that matched the DC-3's speed and opened a 2X2 foot door at the rear for the camera to protrude. Takeoff was again 3:00 a.m. because we wanted morning light on the face of the mountain behind the subject aircraft. It's wonderful how many things there are to learn in life. When you fly along the face of a mountain, the subject aircraft flying side by side with the camera aircraft are subjected to violent downdrafts that curl over the mountain to bump, shake and rattle you in a frightening manner and make the assistant cameraman lose his breakfast.

The director's job was preparing and passing barf bags - in for empty, out for full. We shot a lot of film and did not have a piece of useable product longer than two seconds. We came close to disaster when a violent down draft threw the two planes towards each other. That moment saved the day. The DC-3 panicked and peeled away. The shot of the DC-3 peeling away was smooth and useable.

We were on time.

Back in Toronto, a superb craftsman had prepared models of the supersonic aircraft and the landing port.

The production house rented a defunct pipe factory because there wasn't a studio large enough to do the job. Crew prepared a huge star field by poking holes in black back-drops and aligning hundreds of lights behind. The hero of the set construction however, was the set painter who painted the moons. The largest moon was a 40-foot circular structure, mounted high in the studio on which our hero painted moon craters with spray guns. He had not been told where the light source was going to come from, so he painted one side of the moon with shadows on the left and the opposite side with shadows on the right.

Genius.

The cut spot read well. Shown on the air, the only complaints were #1- next time you choose to zip about in the air over Canmore, (Banff National Park) wait until after breakfast please. #2- A complaint from an antique car buff in Saskatchewan claimed the Ford sedan parked beside the waving wife had two, too many chrome strips in its grill for the year it portrayed.

The woman who loaned the shoot her antique tablecloth got it back without damage and a little money to boot.

The antique car club removed two strips of metal from the 1937 Ford sedan.
To view Share our Tomorrows access williamirish.info

Productions & Executions

Canada's Last Cigarette Commercial.

Allan Sneath worked for McKim Advertising in Montreal. McKim was Canada's oldest advertising agency and had been responsible for many effective communicating concepts including Canada's first bank ads.

The director received a phone call from Allan Sneath on Saturday. He requested the director be on a plane to Calgary on Monday with a cameraman, a film crew and a pair of running shoes because the commercials he had to shoot must be completed very quickly. An explanation on the plane included the information that a person, who watched the activities of American-owned Marlboro Cigarettes for Canadian-owned Imperial Tobacco, had on that day, warned Imperial Tobacco that Marlboro was going to introduce their popular cigarettes into Canada. A strong and well advertised brand name like Marlboro would do Imperial Tobacco's brands considerable damage. The 'spy' who seemed to have very specific information, claimed Marlboro's first step would be to run test commercials to prove the brand's worth in Peterborough, Ontario.

Allan Sneath's job was to make three competing commercials, to run in Peterborough at the same time as Marlboro's. The Marlboro images were of very strong, healthy Montana cowboys riding, roping and living in the outdoors. Allan's plan was to make commercials with images of strong, healthy, Alberta cowboys. Marlboro had the advantage of time but Imperial Tobacco had an interesting advantage of its own. A smart Imperial executive had, long ago, purchased the rights to the name Marlboro in Canada. If the American Marlboro was going to invade Canada, they would have to give their product a different name.

The U.S. settled on the name Maverick. Allan Sneath's commercials for Imperial Tobacco could carry the name Marlboro. The Americans put the name Maverick on the papers of their Marlboro cigarettes. Imperial Tobacco rewrapped one of their other cigarettes in a Marlboro paper and put them in a brand new Marlboro package.

Meanwhile, in a field at the Rafter Six Ranch near Canmore Alberta, the director was in an old truck as the crew shot a stampede of thirty horses supervised by two handsome cowboys. With that segment completed, they raced over to the Kananaskis River to film a pack train of mountain horses, led by the same two cowboys.

The following morning, the director and his crew arrived early at Horseshoe Canyon near Drumheller. They pulled into the viewpoint above the canyon at 3:00 a.m. to catch a sunrise that was to appear at 4:30 a.m. At 4:00 in the morning, the camera, crew and cowboy were ready but the man with the single sheep that the story needed, had not arrived - at least the worried director didn't think he had. Finally in a desperate state, he went over to the only other car in the parking area and woke the man who was sound asleep at the wheel. "Of course I have the sheep," he said. "It's in the trunk." When the trunk was opened, a sheep that had never seen a car before, became airborne. The sheep owner fought the leaping, bouncing, frantic animal down into the canyon, found a few blades of grass, tethered it and left it to recover.

The story the filmmakers were shooting was about a handsome cowboy who looked all day for a lost sheep.

The sun was an inch above the horizon when the cowboy spotted the sheep and rode towards it. The sheep that had never seen a car, had also never seen a horse. As the large dark thing with a man-thing on top approached, the sheep pulled its stake and ran for its life. It should be mentioned that in addition to the problems the director already had, the horse had never seen a sheep! When the sheep bolted south, the horse bolted north. The cowboy was good at his job; he rode the horse to submission, then gently led it to the patch where the sheep had been tied to a large stone. The cowboy turned to the harried director. "If you would bring the sheep and give me five minutes, I will make it possible for you to finish your shot." Everyone was thrilled. Ten minutes later, the sheep was lifted and placed in the arms of the cowboy.

Asking everone to step back, he proceeded to walk in circles around the nervous horse. The smell of the sheep began to mix with the smells of the man and the sheep/man that was walking circles around him, became less frightening. The horse calmed and the man/sheep moved closer until the cowboy was rubbing the sheep back and forth along the horse, again mixing smells. The cowboy spoke quietly. "Roll the camera please," and hearing the camera start, he gently lifted the sheep onto the horse's withers, then swung aboard behind it.

The rising sun was only a little bit past where it should be for sunset.

The commercials were edited in time and sent from Toronto to Peterborough. The Canadian Marlboro packs were placed on store shelves on the same day as the American Maverick cigarettes. The two conflicting commercials were shown on Peterborough TV stations, also on the same day. Smokers were confused and both products were dead in a week. The Americans withdrew. Their attempt to launch a cigarette into the Canadian market had failed. The Marlboro name went back to bed in a vault in Montreal.

Mr. Sneath was a happy man.

Productions & Executions

The Good Bad & the Ugly

Children aged three to five were chosen, one by one and carefully tested for their verbal skills and personal charm. The casting took two days and an interesting mix of performers was engaged. One curly haired three-year-old decided she didn't like this "casting" thing and she wasn't going to say a word to anyone, no matter what. She didn't, but the director asked that she be included because in a cut of ten kids, a curly haired nod from an angel might spark a moment. The director lay on his stomach, in a pile of pillows. The camera, placed on rails behind him, tracked left and right and was aimed just over his head. When the children responded to him they appeared to be speaking to the camera. A second camera on rails was ready and loaded for the moments when the first camera would run out of film. They shot for 2 days, a new child every fifteen minutes. Kodak stock spiked on day 2. The Agency and the client had agreed on what they wanted the children to say. The children came to the shoot without knowledge of what they were going to be asked, in order to be free of mother rehearsed lines.

The director asked the children to tell him with their own words what having a cold felt like and after they did their best with that, he gave them the words the agency wanted to hear. The little lady, who would not speak in casting, heard the camera roll and immediately told the story of her life and a few too many and too-private, family stories. The editor cut three 15-second spots and one 30-second spot on Miss Curly all by herself. When the editor made his choice of the moments that expressed the children's feelings best, it was discovered there was not a single scripted word included in the cut. The kids stole the show with new and unique ways to explain what a cold felt like.

The director was continually charmed by the children. He asked a little girl how old she was. She looked puzzled for a moment then raise

her arm and popped first one finger, then another, then a third finger and explained that she was "Pwactithing to be fowah". A slightly older performer looked distressed when asked what he was going to be when he grew up. With a look of disdain he answered, "an adult." The director was complimented on the choice of children and asked how he made his choices. He explained that first he didn't make the choices alone. The Agency always had professional opinions and were right as many times as he was. He explained that his own personal system was to check to see if the adult with the child was clean. After that, he checked the willingness of the child to make steady eye contact. How closely would the child approach the director when asked to do so? How large was the child's territorial imperative? How did the parent treat the child? Once, the director did not think the boy the Agency preferred, could do the job. The director pouted a little but did as he was asked. Bell's Agency people in this instance were very right, the young man was able and consistent.

Sometimes on the time-limited shoot day, the exact expectations of a client or Agency cannot be realized because reality rears its ugly head and something has to be adjusted to use the time well. Most agencies have people who are experienced professionals who can accept a rational change. All directors have seen some who can not.

On a Trans Canada Telephone shoot, a child was prompted to cry by a supposedly accidental spill of ice cream onto her pretty dress. The resulting cry was so heart-breaking, everyone immediately agreed to cheer her up and find another solution. Three little girls were required to skip. The shorts of one child kept slipping – it made a much better shot when she jumped, jumped, yanked, jumped, jumped and yanked.

The cowboys and the group of wild horses were going to do a stampede. They waited while a cloud entered the valley, on a shot where sunshine was required. The cloud proceeded to the middle of the valley and came to a stop. Over an entire hour it gradually diminished in size until only a tiny piece of cloud covered the sun.

The time for the shot had passed and no one thought to invent an alternative.

The men who were employed by Ford to do the preparation of cars for photography were their own bosses and their own worst enemies. The camera was placed, the crew ready and the sun was setting. The car preparers chose to prep both sides of the car on a shot that was to shoot only one side. In spite of the screaming director, they approved the car for shooting shortly after the sun had set.

A frequent blunder on a commercial shoot takes place when someone in authority asks the director to try a bright idea that just popped into his/her mind. Few understand that when they ask for that idea to be shot, they immediately lose the shot the director had planned that enhanced the story or product display. The director is very aware of the time he has to complete his shots. If he saves a little time, he will usually have something stored away that he wants to shoot to fill in that piece of time.

The storyboard showed the lovers ambling through a light forest. The production company found the forest and completed the shoot. On their way back to St. John's, they passed a huge grassy area. The cars screeched to a stop, everyone tumbled out. Because of the previously undiscovered beauty of the location, they shot the entire commercial again. Back in Montreal, the client approved the spot without question and never knew he had two.

Productions & Executions

A Fine and Productive Failure.

It was a big shoot, 25 crew members, 10 talent and 5 or 6 assorted manager types, two trucks, one full of bits for factory mechanics, the other full of shiny new Skidoo snowmobiles. The small travelling community moved to Denver Colorado, climbed local roads past Loveland Pass and up to Steamboat Springs. From Steamboat Springs, they climbed to the Continental Divide and set up camp in snow that was more than ten feet deep. The locals loved us, we were fresh money and we were "Skidoo People". The local Skidoo and Mountain Rescue Unit served as our location guides and transporters. The Canadians learned a new trick when the Americans attached inverted car hoods to the skidoos to haul stuff around.. The hoods slithered behind skidoos carrying hay bales, humans and anything and everything the crew needed.

A special bonding took place between the Bombardier mechanics and the Rescue Unit. The challenge of the Wild & Wooly Rescue Unit was to surpass a fellow who had managed a 360 degree rotation inside an ice tunnel on a local mountain. The trick required an enhanced machine and the Bombardier mechanics helped the rescuers pump their machines by adding and subtracting items that magnified engine power. The result of the increase in power was a rider who jumped a car and broke both his ankles, and a cross-the-field blind rooster tail, accomplished by travelling at extreme speeds under powder snow.

The adrenaline hit provided by all the physical activity enhanced testosteronicle activity. Fortunately or otherwise, the bar at the hotel included a permanent feature locally known as the Steamboat Pump. It was her heartfelt purpose in life to entertain all passing crews with robust intimacy.

A location hunt, by snow machine, introduced us to nearby features like sunrise and sunset vistas, picturesque tree lined trails, a hot-spring pool and sharp-tongued locals who didn't approve of the snowmobiles.

When the shoot finally lifted itself out of its distractions and went to work, it included a full variety of interesting shots and some unusual moments such as the bare-faced rider who was asked to do a fast, travelling shot early in the morning. The resulting film showed a man who was a nice rosy pink in the opening moments of the shot and an expressionless, purple mask with white spots, at the end. Another moment showed an agile Skidoo driver leap from his machine and magically disappear. He had jumped too close to a tree where the snow was not packed and sank to his chin in a sea of white.

We had come to this place to shoot seven 30-second spots. Well into the fourth spot, a manager from Bombardier arrived to see how things were going. He was standing on the Robin Nodwell Tracked Carrier and asked if he could look through the camera. This intrusion is often offered to cooperative participants. When the man got his eye to the eyepiece and the assistant cameraman showed him what a zoom lens would do, the man was overcome with film fever and blurted "I have to direct this." The director was willing and the experiment was proceeding well, when the approaching sound of a powerful machine drew everyone's attention.

The new arrival was a Bombardier marketing man from Montreal. He had come to tell the shoot the latest marketing research revealed all possible new sales for that year would be completed by tomorrow. Why produce expensive advertising for something it was unlikely anyone was going to buy?

The Pump waved goodbye as she eyed an arriving cluster of jovial males. The director threw back his last, salt-on-the-rim thing and the mobile community headed back to T.O. Commercials were cut but never shown.

When the crew arrived home, an emotional crew member burst into tears and confessed all to his waiting wife. She was very upset and made it her task to tell the wife of every husband on the shoot. Marriages exploded, friends became enemies. Men entered into wife-imposed slavery and the fellow who had told all...disappeared.

Productions &Executions

Animal Tendencies

He had begun as an art director in an Agency where he produced concepts and graphic answers to marketing problems. When he chose to move to a film production house, he opened a door for the accumulation of further skills. In his new job as studio gopher and sweeper, he asked the owner of the studio if he could set up and load a camera each evening. He arrived each morning at 4.00 a.m. and used the camera to produce still life sequences until 8.00 a.m. At eight o'clock, he picked up his broom and began his day's work. A still life, each morning for two weeks produced eight, 30-second spots that were useable and six that were discarded. He had learned that failure was his best way to knowledge. The reel went out the following week although his first response took a month to arrive.

After three still life jobs, a nice one for Timex, someone gave him a still life shoot with a person in it. Word went out - he could do people! He shot silent vignettes for a long time. Then a vignette arrived with two people in it who spoke to each other. Surprise, dialogue. Away he went.

He didn't beat the heck out of anyone for a couple of years but he had won a spot on the roster. An early still life shot had a mouse in it. From this he learned that mice did not answer to commands and they pooped every seven feet, six if you yelled at them. Later when he was asked if he could handle animals, he always answered "yes" and hired a good animal trainer.

The job was for toilet tissue and involved a white cat. Ms. White Cat would be asked to rise from a soft cushion, in a half, bubble-glass chair, and leap to the edge of a white, fur-encased bathtub. After a leisurely stroll along the tub and passage through a white glass forest of modern shapes, she was to find the Facelle bathroom tissue on the white carpeted floor and rub her body on it in appreciation of its softness. Cats can be trained

to do only one thing at a time. They will do the one thing only if they are hungry and once rewarded they will look at you with disdain if you ask them to do a second activity. The production company accessed a California animal trainer and gave him a month to come up with four identical white cats each of whom would be willing to do one piece of the action. Early on the shoot day, the cats arrived in four wire cages. One of the cages with a gold star on the front, indicated this was the star creature that had been trained to rub herself on the Facelle package.

Surprisingly, it went well but very slowly because the film stock of the time required a perfect balance when shooting white on white. A problem that arose during one of the sequences gifted the director with a new piece of animal knowledge. One of the cats refused to pause where she was required to pause. The animal trainer stepped forward and at the right moment blew gently on the cat's face. The cat looked a bit offended but stopped where she was supposed to stop. Departing the stage, the trainer was heard to say, "It works even better if you've had garlic for lunch."

About 11.00 p.m. they arrived at the cage with the star on it, removed the perfect and final creature, and placed her a few steps away from the colour corrected hero package. On "action," Ms. Cat walked forward with the camera rolling and arrived at the perfect package. She looked it up and down, leapt to the studio floor, found a practice package fresh from the store shelf and rubbed herself all over it. She turned and looked at her viewers as though to say "O.K. now feed me." She had been taught on a store pack not a colour corrected pack. After a break, intended to help her get a little hungrier, a small piece of food was placed on the edge of the colour-corrected package and she was put at her start position. When the camera rolled, she looked up at the people around her and seemed to say, "My union will hear about this," then stepped forward and sniffed the food on the pack. The editor, on the section of the shot where the cat stretched out to sniff the food, ran it forward and backward and forward and backward.

Ms. Cat returned to her Hollywood mansion.

Productions &Executions

Memories

He can't remember the product to be advertised. Of the more than two thousand commercial productions he remembers in detail, this production's product has disappeared. The shoot required a winding rural road that was poorly maintained, with dips where the 1950's vintage car disappeared, and little hills it could pop over and occasionally, a nice corner it could swish around. He remembers a man with a pencil moustache driving but can't remember why.

The location finders had given up so the director had gone looking. Three days later he found half a road and towards dusk, the other half a mile away. The shoot began with a 500 mm lens that painted the frame with out-of-focus grasses and interesting shapes. The long lens also had the effect of squaring things up, the car looked attractive, the driver a bit chubby. Maybe the shoot was about overweight males, maybe a health issue... gone.

The car was a very attractive, warm tan, 1950's De Soto with disappearing headlights. It was in mint condition on the outside and the interior looked as if it had never been touched. The speedometer read 2,482 miles. The reason the car had gone such a short distance is a story that comes with the car.

Three spinster sisters had lived together in the house in which they were born, near London, Ontario. The three were very happy with the way things were and never went hunting for men or trouble; they were self sufficient and never complained. They were social, went to church, local events, political speeches and community gatherings. One day, one of the ladies expressed the desire to indulge in a vacation. The other two agreed and a great discussion ensued about where they would go and how. Bus tours, sailing ships, ranch style getaways, all types and methods of travel were gleefully considered in their deliberations.

In the end, they decided to buy a brand new DeSoto automobile, learn to drive and do the 2,485 mile round trip to a good hotel in Florida. The trip was marvelous; they could not believe how much fun it was to visit a brand new place and use their new driving skills. They made it there and back without a driving error and bang-on the budget they had chosen. Two days after their arrival home, the youngest sister died. It was a normal, understandable passing; still the two older sisters were heart broken. They left the car untouched in the driveway where they had parked it when they returned from Florida.

One evening, the oldest sister phoned a friend whose husband ran a construction company. Two days later, a construction crew removed the west wall of the living room, built a ramp and drove the DeSoto into a space next to the piano. The ramp was removed and the wall repaired. The engine was never started again while the ladies were alive. The two sisters would often sit in the car beside the piano to remember their sister and recount the stories of their happy trip. When the remaining two sisters died, the house was sold and the car removed and sold for a good price to a man who kept vintage cars for film sequences.

Productions & Executions

Disasters Unlimited

The director helped to choose the child. The child's mother had brought him to the casting where it was immediately obvious he was bright and personable, and at three, seemed beyond his years. He didn't have a runny nose or the usual bumps and bruises of a three year old. The set was constructed in Toronto in a time when the benefit of sets over location was appreciated. It was a nice construction job; the set company had saved an early staircase and railing from the demolition man and put walls and supports around the stairs. The design supported the idea that the family we were about to reveal, was reasonably well-to-do.

It took two hours to light and prop. Then the camera rolled and the carefully chosen child appeared at the top of the stairs and began his slow descent. He was dressed in little boy nightwear that had feet attached and everyone was in love by the time he reached the bottom. His job, when he got down the stairs, was to run to the centre of the room and hug his father who lay on the couch with an open newspaper on his chest. Perfect. The little fellow threw himself on his father; father sat up and hugged the child. To everyone's surprise, the father, who was supposed to greet the little boy, instead began to scream. He screamed at the top of his lungs and screamed and screamed, attempting all the time to remove the child from his lap. Everyone rushed forward and saw that the little boy had the man's left breast in his teeth and was biting with enthusiasm. The shoot was closed while the bleeding actor went to the hospital for attention.

It was decided not to continue and the product that needed a little boost from a commercial with a little boy never got the boost. When asked why he bit the man, the boy replied, "Nobody asked me if I wanted to do this stuff" and burst into tears.

To the southeast of fabulous Mount Assinaboine, there is a high ridge that affords the best view of its soaring peak. The helicopter approached the ridge with great care because the pilot knew that ridges frequently had gusting winds racing up their sides. The chopper sat down carefully on a rounded piece of mountain top, cliffs front and back. It was about the size of a living room. The pilot explained to the three dismounting members that they had five minutes, while he remained at the controls and kept the machine running. After a short discussion about the value of the location, the three climbed back on board and the amazing machine eased into the air. The discussion undertaken on the mountain top had been about the value of using this high spot as a camera position for shooting images of Molson-employed cliff climbers.

The conversation concluded that as beautiful as the shot was, the helicopter supply of equipment and crew was too easily interrupted by wind. If the weather soured, the production could have members stranded on a mountain top. After their stop on the ridge, the chopper took them to the centre-front of the mountain and climbed to a height where they could look down on the face.

Suddenly, instead of the rhythmic thump of the helicopter blades, there was silence. A sharp down draught had taken the grab out of the blades and the craft plummeted vertically for about five hundred feet. The fellow positioned at the port door had forgotten to do up his safety belt. He did it up very quickly. The client who sat behind the column-like propeller shaft leaned forward and threw both arms firmly around it. The director, who sat at the starboard door, lost the blood supply to his face. When it could grab air again, the blades bent upwards like a bow and the chopper body stressed enough to pop open the side doors. Open doors left the two outside passengers with a frightening straight down view of a cold mountain lake. The pilot suggested firmly that the group return to base. The location chosen later was a little cliff beside a road. It did look like a big cliff when they chose the correct angle to shoot it from. The masculine Molson performers looked good on the cliff and were never placed in danger.

Productions & Executions

Glutinous Fruition

The amazing result of the property manager's (props) labours was a luminous fruit tree that grew huge fruit of every variety that Jell-O ever made. A peach for instance, was ten inches in diameter and sat on flat milk-glass plates cut to fit the fruit. If it had been tried on a real tree, the leaves would have been too small, so the prop man taped about two thousand flat green leaves onto the branches. When the director looked at it, he had a problem. "Light passes through leaves and looks much more lively than those flat green leaves." So the prop man began again, cutting and gluing and using a transparent paper. The tree was finally assembled, turned on its side so it could be viewed from the top and small lights could be placed under the fruit to make them glow deliciously. The camera was fixed to a platform high in the studio grid about 30 feet from the tree. A long lens helped to hide the lights hidden under the fruit and erased the flare around the edges. It was decided that a full test was required, so the dietician arrived with fruit-shaped moulds filled with Jell-O.

The first test took a day to construct and was performed in a cold studio to keep the Jell-O firm. The cinematographer climbed to the roof, a light switch was flipped and the test began. In the time it took the cameraman to check his exposures, multiple mayhem ensued. The fruit was warmed by the small lights under their platform and gleefully slid to the studio floor. Some bounced and rolled, others broke into vibrating segments.

For the second test, it was decided to double the gelatin and remove the flavour. The production enjoyed its second failure with a hail of fruit that did not splat and vibrate but bounced and rolled gleefully on the floor. Test #3. went forward with some confidence; a thicker under-plate was put in place for each fruit to keep the light from warming the gelatin and making the surface of the under-plate a bit harder to slide on. Now each fruit felt, bounced and tasted very much like a soccer ball.

"Take a chance and shoot the damn thing," said an unidentified voice. We did and so began the days of the Jell-O Tree as a symbol of the great variety of flavours for the longest standing, and most profitable, product in North America.

With each commercial, there were shots of children enjoying a bowl of Jell-O. In the first spot, a very handsome, square headed, blonde, blue-eyed boy, probably four or five, was asked if he enjoyed the flavour. "Oh, yes!" he replied, "I really like it." It was learned later that a mistake was made by the props person and the little boy had been given pure soccer ball gelatin with bright Jell-O colour but no flavour.

The product was so popular that the word Jell-O became a generic name for gelatin deserts.

There are more than 158 Jell-O branded products and about 300 million boxes of Jell-O are sold in the U.S. each year.

Vodka and rum are used in Jell-O drinks. The musical South Pacific began the saying, "Life is just a bowl of Jell-O."

In 1992, a woman won a Nobel Prize in chemistry for inventing blue Jell-O.

Women wrestlers wrestle in green Jell-O.

Productions &Executions

Caring

A job's success or demise is often decided by the people who bring it to the production unit.

The Detroit advertising agency did promotion work for Canadian Tire. The young man, who wrote the spot for the Agency, was certain that he had written a spot that would solve Canadian Tire's problem. He was right. His producer sent out the Agency storyboard and asked several production companies to quote. After careful consideration and the submission of a director's board, the Agency chose Partners Film Company in Toronto.

On the first casting session, a long lanky folk musician was chosen for his appearance and easy going nature. When asked what he had done in the area of past performances, he said he had done some very good animal sounds and his area of speciality was chickens. The search for a son that had ability and fit the father, encompassed seven major Canadian cities and was not successful until a gawky little kid turned up on a Vancouver tape. The director had asked that they travel to Saskatchewan for the perfect place to shoot this perfect story but there just wasn't that kind of money. He searched on his weekends for a spot that had slipped out of the West and was living in Ontario. Driving west out of Uxbridge along the height of land between Lakes Ontario and Simcoe, he spotted a promising hill and drove up to the farm house to ask permission for the production company to use the property. Unfortunately, the person who owned the farm was a German Baron and he did not like the director or film companies. Dismissed, dismayed and deflated, the director headed for Toronto. Half way there, the idea hit him. "Who owned the other side of that hill?" The other side of the hill was also owned by the Baron but the production didn't need to put a foot on it. They could use it as a Saskatchewan backdrop. The next day, the director sent a handsome and engaging production manager to ask permission from the lady who owned the neighbouring property.

Upon the young man's success, the director walked the property, carefully setting his shots. The following day, he stayed home and drew a detailed map of where the fence was to be constructed, where the road was to be cut in the grass and where the barn would be built. In setting these pieces of the story, he made the assumption that he would have a perfect day to shoot his spot and would be able to shoot everything in back-lit situations. The story would be more romantic back-lit and he believed in weather forecasts.

Shoot day and the sun was under a light cloud. Instead of shooting compromised exteriors (how could he when the young writer had his hopes so high), the director rehearsed in places the camera would be when they began to shoot in the afternoon. This risky trick allowed the afternoon shoot of noon to 7.00 PM, to be completed very quickly and to be better lit. When the last shot arrived, the director realized he had trapped himself. He had just shot the father lifting the bike from the truck, back lit. That meant that if the director's rules were to be followed, he had to shoot the boy's reaction to the bike - front lit. The cameraman heard the director fussing and said "Your sun is setting, so shoot!" The director cheated and shot the boy's moment of awestruck surprise, back lit. Nobody even noticed. On the first take of the boy's surprised response, the door to the van in which they had placed the client's monitor, flew open. The director's heart sank because he knew the shot just taken was exactly what he wanted (good kid) and what he saw was the writer running towards him with a revision. Damn. The young writer arrived at the director's side. "That was perfect; please don't shoot another version." Then to complicate things, a person of importance, in the last seconds of the setting sun, insisted on the boy riding into the sunset. Knowing that an appendage to his job description was *'slave to the money source,'* the director shot the boy and the sunset. It should be noted that the POI had the good sense not to insist on the inclusion of his shot in the final cut.

An able and experienced editor recognized the enthusiasm of the young agency writer and worked two days and several nights to achieve a perfect cut. Bessies competition gave it a gold.

Productions & Executions

A Crew for all Seasons

Molson was a frequent client; the director liked the simplicity of the jobs and the number of times Molson had to pay him his director's fee. Directors were paid a nice chunk for the day they shot but nothing for the days they did research, sales, desk work or prepared detailed organization for a production. A single shoot day took an average of ten days of intense preparation, so divide the director's fee by eleven and you arrive at an amount a bit better than a plumber and a lot less than a corporate manager. Directors however, have much more fun. They have their problems refreshed with new ones every day, and meet many more 'hands on' difficulties than a manager.

Big Bald Lake was finally decided to be the best spot to shoot. Big Bald is a northern extension of Pigeon Lake. The spit of land the production needed turned out to be on aboriginal territory. Negotiations with the First Nation people proved positive and they allowed the unit to use a point of land that stuck into Big Bald's middle. The point of land gave the production a place to mount the camera in order to shoot across a small bay, and feature fall colour of *Group of Seven* character on the opposite side. The location could not be accessed by land, so a platoon of boats was supplied by a nearby resort.

The concept of the Big Bald Lake commercial was that the ingestion of a Molson beer was a pleasant experience summer, fall or winter. The job for the camera crew was to design and construct a single unending shot that travelled through all of those seasons. Dolly rails were run on a narrow wooden platform for about fifty feet around rocks and under branches. The year-long dolly was marked in foot measurements next to the rails, then a practice dolly-move translated feet into feet-per-second and all of these measurements were marked on the platform floor. The crew practiced the three season run several times, then covered the winter portion so snow could be easily removed. As soon as all was perfection, the summer, one-third portion of the camera move, was shot.

A local fellow was hired to keep an eye on the platform. He put up a sign that read "Beware Pet Cougar." Everything was loaded in boats and returned to the resort for transport. The footage was examined by the Agency in Toronto and accepted.
In the fall, the crew drove out to Big Bald Lake and found the location in good condition. The leaves had not yet fully reached the height of their colour but would do so soon. A phone call informed the production unit that the autum portion of the camera move had to be shot immediately for undefined reasons.

Everyone was designated a volunteer props person and given a can of paint. More ladders arrived and branches with leaves that couldn't be reached by a brush on a stick, were hidden by the addition of coloured branches. It was a little shabby and all agreed nature could have done a better job. On approval, dolly andcamera rolled down the next portion of the Molson railway and the second portion was accepted.

Summer and fall were joined by an editor's dissolve and all agreed the concept worked. Winter arrived and the crew unloaded at the resort and worked their way to the location. After a check on the ice, the camera equipment, the dolly and rails were driven down the lake in a Jeep and a box truck. No one could put a foot on the pristine scene, so a circuitous entry to the platform was made with the equipment. A tent was set up behind the track for the care and attention of a young man and a gorgeous young woman who were to ski through the scene as the camera moved along on its winter portion. The young woman chosen for the shot was a popular performer and when the Agency executive spotted her, he made the unfortunate decision to go into the warming tent and entertain her. The closer he got to her, the more engrossed he became. He took one too many steps and placed himself in front of the flame-thrower heater. There was a loud WHUMPH and his winter pull-over pants went away. He left the shoot carefully trying to hold together the loose insulation which was all that remained of the pants. As he disappeared from sight, a loud CRACK was heard and the Jeep slithered to a forty-five degree angle, half in and half out of the lake. A small conference concluded that the weather was threatening but the shoot had to go ahead.

Two men were released to get the Jeep out of the lake. *Gorgeous Couple* skied through the scene, camera functioned well in the winter weather and the call of "cut and print" was heard simultaneously with a pop and gurgle sound, as the equipment truck joined the Jeep in the lake.
The story should have ended there and it did for the performers, executives and camera crew. They wandered off home, but the grips, production assistants and gophers stayed for three days. Chain saws were acquired and the Jeep released from ice that had wanted to keep it for the season. The equipment truck was judged to be too firmly fixed in place. A large crane was brought onto the lake. For its safety, the crane's legs were extended and sheets of plywood placed under each foot to spread the weight and prevent it from joining the truck. A cable was attached to the truck, the crane pulled, the ice broke and the crane and the plywood joined the truck in the lake. The director wasn't there to see the end of the story. It is believed a smaller crane and a larger crew who were expert at pulling things from lakes, got everything up from the bottom, except the wounded pride of the production house and their crew.

Productions
&Executions

Wonder Kids

The most difficult part of many shoots is casting. For each casting session, the director sat in a small room with Agency creative, producers and a person on a video camera, to interview one hundred and fifty kids from ten o'clock in the morning to seven o'clock at night. Everyone suffered more than the director because the director was continually challenged to respond to the things that came out of the youthful mouths. He didn't have time to worry about the cramp in his leg or the pain in his behind. He sat on an apple box that gave him the same eye level as the kids. The box was close to the children, allowing him clear eye contact and a chance to see if the children were interested or afraid. Some children felt no fear and the only difficulty was getting them to stop talking. One very young lady explained to the room that her mother had a new boyfriend and her daddy didn't know "anything" about it. One child answered "No" to every question. Another offered only a magnificent pout. If the children's conversations were not always on target, they were consistently interesting. When siblings came in together, one would answer the questions for both of them. Twins were particularly prone to this. Big sisters told the room all the things their little brother wanted to say. Some children took a look at the room full of staring eyes and burst into tears. 'First-time' kids were applauded, sometimes it worked, often not. Kids who only made it to the door before panic set in, were asked to come back when they were ready.

The first set of commercials for Wonderbread included the use of twins to demonstrate how similar the whole wheat loaf looked to the white bread loaf. On camera, the children examined the two kinds of slices to see if they could identify a difference. This was followed by a shot of two identical children holding up identical bread and saying, "They're identical." The commercial was completed successfully and market share and public comment popped nicely.

The director was asked how he withstood a day full of children. "The easy answer is I don't have to take them home. A better answer is their refreshing way of expressing things."

Later Wonderbread work included commercials for the Vancouver Olympics. The shoots were designed for a large number of shots; always the children had fun showing the crew the amazing things they could do. Two boys in full gear, raced down a ski slope, knees bending in unison, snow flying by. In fact they stood in place, bending their knees to take the imaginary bumps as the crew used a fan to blow snow past them.

The boys in the bobsled had the most fun, especially when the sled escaped down an imaginary hill and they had to run after it. A little man named Noah, who wore thick glasses, had a good feeling for the moment. When the sled was released, he was overcome by excitement and leapt into the air. Everything was shot in a white studio. Kids were brought to the set in one hour units. The director was pleased - no wounds, no complaints, good results.

Over the years, the director has had the pleasure of meeting many intelligent and uninhibited children and acknowleges the gift they have given him. A Bell Telephone spot found a young man (ten) who was sure he could do the job. The director wasn't sure but listened to the Agency writer who liked the child. The job won attention at the Bessies principally because of the abilities of the young man. Years later on a flight to Montreal, an attractive woman passenger came down the aisle, bent to the director and asked if he was Mr. Irish. When he confirmed that he was, she said, " Please, come with me." He did, and was taken to a mid-aircraft seat and introduced to a handsome young man of eighteen who was on his way to university. The director was mystified. The woman said, "He's your Bell Telephone boy."

Kraft had a spot for their cheese slices that included a five-year-old in a yellow raincoat and a yellow hat. His name was B.J. and when he reached up for the mailbox slot, he was a bit short. When he stretched up on his tiptoes and did his best to get the damn letter in the slot, all viewing parents fell in love. B.J. was featured in several commercials, once with his dad, fixing the car.

Another, with his pretend mom reading a bed-time story for Kraft. If asked what B.J. stood for, he would look surprised and reply, "B.J."

In a Mr. Christie Book Award commercial, the director, in spite of his most devious tricks, was unable to draw the right actions from a four-year-old boy with Down Syndrome. The child was supposed to lie on his stomach and look at a book. The director struggled until a beautiful, five-year-old blonde pushed him aside, threw herself down beside the boy and said, "Oh my, look at that!" the boy rolled over onto his stomach and proceeded to do exactly what the director needed. The beautiful blonde turned out to be the little boy's sister and she prompted wonderful responses from him.

A first time and very young performer listened carefully to the director as he explained the things that he was required to do. The director explained that he was required to stand in his costume, on his mark, and examine a box of Mr. Christie's cookies. The shot went well and everyone broke for lunch. After lunch at the next location, panic broke out when the little boy could not be found. A thorough search discovered him standing patiently and alone, with his toes exactly on the mark at the morning's location.

For the Ontario Milk Marketing Board some years ago, the job required a child to have a bath in a half-barrel filled with warm water. The barrel was prepared, the temperature tested and a cooperative little girl stepped in.

Her name was Megan Follows.

Productions & Executions

The Terminator

Christmas was closing fast, the large retail corporation was in a hurry and a lack of detail was excused. Approval was given to two concepts, a sales situation in-store and an incident that included Rudolph the Red-Nosed Reindeer.

Quotes went out. Many areas of cost remained afloat. Meetings were held that distressed the director because "hurry" was the purpose and detail ignored. There was an obvious lack of Agency executives - who were busy doing something else - and the creatives were enjoying an unusual amount of freedom. The director was impressed by the freedom but didn't like the information gaps. Not wanting to lose the financial advantage the job would bring, he closed his eyes and plodded on.

The production team was not allowed to shoot in a store so a large set was constructed in studio. On the shoot day, the pretend doors opened and a crowd of performing purchasers rushed in. The camera picked an attractive woman out of the crowd and followed her to a cash counter. Dialogue had never been written for this portion. The director invented a few words suited to the moment. The creative director immediately objected because he wanted that portion of the spot left for a later addition of voice-over words. The explanation made sense and the director conceded. After a few product still life shots, the shoot was wrapped and everyone went home. The shoot for the next day was all night.

The night shoot was set in a grove of pines, in a small valley north of Toronto. The area of pines was chosen because the shoot had to be done before green leaves were gone. An artificial soap-snow was put down over the area and looked very much like winter on the ground and in the trees. Five small trees were dressed with plastic and potato snow and carefully carried here and there as the camera changed position.

The last light of day faded and the crew prepared for the night to follow.

The camera rolled as the subject car appeared, the shot widened slowly to show the full winter scene. In the car, a father, mother and little boy were enjoying the night. As they entered a clearing, a reindeer crossed through the car headlights. In a close-up, we see the face of the boy as it appears in a side window. He is amazed and as a flash of red light reflects in the window, he whirls around to tell his parents the reindeer is Rudolph. To get this much shot, it took from eight at night until three in the morning. The man who had brought the deer claimed him as a pet and swore he could get it to do what was needed. He demonstrated this ability on his farm in the deer's pen. The deer had not agreed however to do as he was told in the black of night, up to his knees in soap.

Several times he stayed in the trees, refusing to come out. Grunting and expletives could be heard in the dark, but the deer won, man lost. Three times the deer crossed the road well out of the cars headlights. Once, to demonstrate his supremacy, the deer dragged his friend and master into the view of the camera and then dragged him back into the bush. It was discovered later that the deer's owner had his sleeve caught on a horn. Rain began and the soap-snow began to disappear.

The boy, who did not have to ride in the car during the wide shots, had been sequestered in comfort in a nearby motel. The only job he had yet to accomplish was to make a comment about the deer to his parents when he whirled around. At three in the morning, in the rain, he was wrapped in a blanket and brought to the car. It took a bit of time to shoehorn the director, cameraman, driver, lighting equipment and boy into their assigned places in the car. When that was finally achieved, the car and the camera rolled together and the boy stared wide-eyed at the camera. He turned his head back and forth, and refused to utter a word.

A final shot of the deer was on the shot list but there was nothing on the list about a deer in pounding rain that had turned snow to bubbles.

Productions &Executions

Sometimes

A commercial out for bids looked good. The commercial was for a product named Novahistex and the Agency was asking for treatments. The director, once he had looked over the Agency script and story board, was discouraged. He thought the Agency treatment was close to perfect and he was certain he would be shown up by some hot-shot director who had a different way to do it. He didn't fight it. He told the Agency not to change any part of the board. He was surprised when the job was given to them the following morning. The director, who considered he was fortunate to be doing what he was doing, did not refuse jobs. As each job came within grabbing distance, he did his best to hook it. He did admit there were some jobs he would rather not do, but accepted them if they were available to him. He felt he did not have the right to turn away a job. Even the bad ones taught him something.

The Novahistex job was a *ten* and a *ten* is harder to do than a *three* because there is no room to improve on a *ten*. If you make a *nine* out of a *ten*, you don't get the next job.

The director made a phone call, packed a bag and drove two days to Halifax. At the Canadian Navy Yards in Halifax, he pulled up to the gate and explained his purpose. The guard made a phone call and when he returned, he showed the director where to park. "Lt. Agnew will be with you shortly." He hoped Lt. Agnew would be late. Ships of many different types grumbled and drooled as they lay tied to iron anvils. Military personnel marched about showing off their perfect posture and perfectly pressed uniforms. It was an observer's paradise. Unfortunately Lt. Agnew was prompt and arrived in five minutes. He walked the director down

the docks and led him into an area that cuddled three, long, black and beautiful submarines. Lt. Agnew and the director crossed a slender angle iron gangplank and stood on the narrow deck of the nearest submarine. While on deck, Lt. Agnew gave a rough outline of the subs, where they came from and their present condition. The one we were standing on was a British diesel, recently purchased from from Britain. "When we go down below you will find that certain objects are covered in canvas because they are parts of processes that are secret."

"Also", he added, "our time below is limited because I have a meeting in ten minutes." Lt. Agnew then disappeared into the body of the cigar-shaped weapon and the director followed. Inside, he was amazed to see how little room there was and how many things were covered in canvas. He did however, achieve a good sense of the shape and mood of the interior of the sub. Nine minutes later the director was shown to a ladder that led to the upper deck and obediently climbed up and waited for Lt. Agnew. Lt. Agnew came up very slowly and on reaching the top explained, "My meeting is with the head of the Navy and I have to make sure I don't arrive with submarine grease on my white shirt." The director assured him that he was indeed spotless, said his thank-you's and departed.

Armed with useful knowledge, the director was able to guide the set design for pieces of a submarine that needed to be seen in the Novahistex spot. All of the secret, hidden pieces were invented by the set company to confuse foreign agents and the shoot proceeded well. The performers were interesting and appropriate in their performance.

There was an interesting result of the shoot and cut. The commercial shown on television matched the Agency storyboard perfectly. The Canadian Television Bessies agreed with the director's assessment and gave Novahistex an "Award of Merit."

Productions &Executions

Rings a Bell

The director often proclaimed to all who would listen that luck and ability are the two most important aspects of a successful production. When he said the word 'luck,' he meant blind good fortune. When he said 'ability' he meant performing artists. There were many times in his years of work that a performer with unusual abilities made the director's approximate skills appear to be amazing.

In the casting session for the Bell Gift Certificate, the director was introduced to an interesting flock of creatives. They fluttered in, all excited with the experience. Their inexperience showed through the cracks in their bravado but they were fair minded and that was all the director required. Children came to the casting session when they were finished with school so the early part of the day was taken with older men who were required as bus drivers. The requirements for the driver was that he be sixty plus and vulnerable. The requirements for the eight to nine year old boy were that he be self assured and able to vocalize. In commercial casting, as opposed to feature casting, it is helpful if the physical appearance of the actor displays some of his character because there is much less time to develop the personality of the performer. A slender gentleman of some age was chosen as the bus driver. The director spoke to him at the casting to make him aware that he might be required in his performance to go as far as shedding a tear. A handsome young man was chosen as the boy. The director was, at first, a bit unsure of the boy but he passed the director's 'territorial' test and confirmed he had the self-confidence to do the job. The boy had stood nose to nose with the director without a quiver.

The Bell Gift Certificate was to be used for a Christmas promotion. In late November, after a few falls of snow, the crew assembled their tools in a valley north of Toronto.

When all was prepared and ready to go, an unfriendly warm spell erased the snow. Focus was turned to the parts of the action that took place inside the bus and two days of warm weather were used to shoot a bus being towed by a truck that shot potato flakes past windows covered in artificial frost. The young man did his job well, as did the driver but the remaining exterior moments had to have snow and were to be covered on the last day of the shoot. The forecast gave little comfort and everyone flopped into bed early and a little dejected. About four o'clock in the morning, the director got up to review his lists, as many directors do, and remembered he had left his glasses in the car. He snuck down the back stairs, under-dressed, in the dark.

The light that was supposed to illuminate the outside of the back door was broken and when the director swung the door open what he saw was a black wall. Tentatively, he stepped out onto the cement pad he knew was there and wondered why his foot made a loud crunch instead of a soft pat. Hoar frost! Holy !@ @! Everything was coated in heavy hoar frost. He woke the production manager and the manager went room to room bashing his fist on doors. Sunlight burns off hoar frost as soon as it strikes it. The critical snow shots had to be done once and quickly. At six o'clock, pre-breakfast, the bus came down the road in a frame of winter white and stopped at the farm driveway. Shot completed. The boy was rushed up the driveway while little patches of first light began to warm the frost. No one could remember what the boy was going to call to the bus driver. The boy did. The only other shot in which snow was required was completed while the white stuff dripped. The snow issue now past, the boy had yet to deliver a paragraph of dialogue, nose to nose, with the bus driver. He did it twice. The boy's ability was confirmed when everyone chose his first delivery.

When all was done the driver looked over at the director. "Are you sure you won't need a tear?" "I brought some old love letters just in case." The director thanked him. "As I watched you, I realized that with an accomplished performer, a brush stroke is more effective than a hammer."

Productions &Executions

S.O.A. and S.O.B.

The director can't remember why he ended up in his favourite part of the country but he was in Calgary when the call came in. While he was there would he mind doing a little spot for Esso and be paid for it? Not even a little bit.

The director was born in Calgary and lived in Edmonton and places in between throughout his high school years. His interest in the rigorous parts of school was low so he viewed it as a necessary recess between his outdoor adventures. He started work on farms when he was thirteen and when he was sixteen, he began a three summer adventure working on trail crews for Canada's first national park in Waterton Lakes, Alberta. During the school year, he found occasions to ride his thumb in whatever direction struck his fancy; consequently he knew Alberta's parts and places very well.

The script and board were faxed through and the moment he saw the board, he knew where he was going to shoot. Two highways went west from Calgary towards Banff, There was an old one with two battered lanes and broken shoulders and a new one with two lanes in each direction and a very wide centre medium. Half way to Banff, the old highway makes a dramatic plunge down the Cochrane Hill. *There were three well-spaced runaway truck lanes with a little boarded up house at the bottom. The fellow who owned the house gave it up after a truck went through the living room when he was in the bath. Another took out the bath when he was in the living room.* Farther along and almost as far as the smallest church in Canada, *an Aboriginal Historic Site*, the old highway makes a nice curve into a gully.

The small crew arrived and the camera was set with a long lens and well back from the curve and the dip. A local had an older car so the production hired him to drive it around the corner and down the hill until it was hidden from sight. Take one was fine and you can't use two. The crew was off to the airport.

In T.O., effects were added after the car disappeared in the gully. The car engine was heard to stutter, cough and quit. The viewer saw only the empty road but heard the rolling vehicle bump and scrape to a stop at the bottom of the gully. There were the sounds of several attempts to start the engine. The door creaked open to release the driver, then slammed shut with energy. The viewer heard some muttered epithets, then a wham! as the driver kicked his car. The sounds of the driver's footsteps were heard walking up the road. Just as the commercial ended, the driver's head was seen bobbing over the rise in the road.

The voice-over message covered the idea that if you haven't had your car checked lately, stop in at an Esso station and have it attended to. The crew called it the "Radio Commercial" because it contained more audio information than visual. The director called it a paid holiday.

A few years later, Esso asked again. The location was a local, Toronto 'full service' gas station. The commercial's idea was that a gas station, in addition to pumping gas, could do effective mechanical services as well. A senior mechanic was shown teaching a junior mechanic the tricks of the trade. The Toronto location meant the Agency creatives were in attendance and at noon, the Agency art director decided to pump the director's enthusiasm by showing him Esso work presently being done in England by another director. At the end of the viewing, the art director turned to the director. "There now, do you think you can do as well as that?" The commercials the director had been shown were huge musical shows, drama spots with budgets in the millions and they did not relate in any way to what was being done for one hundred thousand dollars in a Toronto gas station. The director saw the incident as diminishment and knew he was doing what could be done for the simple story. The director refrained from exploding and finished his day as quickly as he could. He did not do the additional gift shots he had planned because the extra shots would have cost the production company dollars that he was no longer willing to spend on the jerk from the advertising agency.

Productions & Executions

Tak

His name was, and probably still is, Ken Takasaki. He was a writer for McKim in Montreal and wrote for the Bell Telephone account. Ken graduated from a prestigious university in something that got him a good job in a good Agency. He was raised and schooled in Montreal. By the time he graduated from university, his original ethnicity no longer inhabited his mind. The director's introduction to "Tak" was when he was telling a joke to a group of friends. As he neared the punch line, he put a finger on the corner of each eye, pulled the corners downwards and said something in a comedic Japanese accent. Ken had forgotten he didn't need to help his face look Japanese.

Ken phoned the production house, explained the project, then flew to Toronto. Both the director and the cameraman weren't certain how long the spot would take to achieve. They knew if they could sit on the flat prairie for a week or two, they would eventually get it done. Situations like this are financially dangerous. It was suggested by the executive producer that cost plus twenty percent would be the most responsible way to go. It wasn't as though there were huge costs involved; all that was required was a director, cameraman, producer and Ken. All they had to do was stay in a bad motel in Medicine Hat and do a single shot for Bell Telecommunications.

Bell needed a shot in which the sun came over a sharp edged, cloud free horizon, rose and placed its perfect circle behind the top of the Telecommunications tower. The perfectly clean horizon would be the first problem. Placing the camera in exactly the right spot so the sun would hit the tower perfectly, was the second problem. The sun does not accommodate everyone by coming up vertically. It comes up at an angle to the horizon and that angle changes every day of the year.

The third problem was the size of the sun. We couldn't order a fat sun for Thursday to be big enough to surround the tower. We had to use a "long" lens to enlarge the sun.

The tower chosen to be the subject of our problems sat on flat prairie, a few kilometres west of Medicine Hat, Alberta. The mighty South Saskatchewan ambled along in a modest canyon, a short distance south of the camera position. The position was found through the simple process of driving away from the tower, until it was the right size on a lens that one guessed would make the sun large enough to surround the tower. The sun's size was defined by pointing various lenses at the sun during the day and finding that something in the order of a five hundred millimetre lens would do the trick.

Permission to set up on the farmer's field was given, with the usual proviso that no one would smoke. The degree on the horizon where the sun would rise was supplied by a local astronomer. The team waited. Three days of cloud provided the team with the pleasure of afternoon matinees and plenty of rest. At three o'clock on the fourth morning, everyone was standing on the flat, equipment at the ready. An unexpected area of the horizon got very hot and everyone grabbed the camera and moved two hundred feet north so the hot area of the horizon was closer to the tower. Everyone stood on their tiptoes in an attempt to see the first glint of light. The glow on the horizon moved through the tower's base and popped the sun up on the wrong side.

The weather held and the next morning the team was back in their original position ready to try again. To better spot the sun's arrival, Tak stood on the car roof. No one was spooked by the horizon glow this time. They all understood the glow that came from below the horizon was from a sun crawling towards the tower at an almost forty-five degree angle. The sun rose from a crisp horizon and passed through the tower. It was just the right size to surround the top of the tower but did not manage to get itself perfectly centred. The weather misbehaved and it was not possible to come back on the following day. The day after that, armed with the careful advice of a mathematician from nearby Sheffield Experimental Station, the crew moved the camera position north, three and a half feet, and east, twenty-seven. Tak had come warmly dressed, carrying seven pillows and a ladder he had borrowed from a startled carpenter. He parked two cars very close together, stuffed the pillows around the ladder to protect the cars, and ascended as far as he could into the perfect blue sky Albertans brag about. "Looks good, looks good," he shouted as glow turned to flash of light and everyone held their breath as the blazing ball rose to the tower and seemed to hold it perfectly centered for half a second.

Bell had its shot.

Tak descended his ladder looking like an overdressed Asian general home from battle.

To get the sunrise shot the crew worked about five hundred feet from and on the flats above this bend in the South Saskatchewan River.

Productions &Executions

A Few Degrees from Perfect

As soon as he heard there was a job in the Yukon, he was up and running.

Coca-Cola had a story about a little girl who was excluded from an outdoor hockey game. Kids pull a toboggan loaded with a Coke cooler and snow shovels, down a country road to the local snow covered lake. The girl follows the group from a distance, feeling diminished and left out even though she knows she is too young to be included in the game. Her shoulders sag, she does her best to be brave. The young leader of the group is handsome and aware of her presence. When they talk, he gives her a Coke and tells her there is a way she can be included. They arrive at the lake and the shovels are put to work in energetic young hands. The rink cleared, they line up in two rows, team facing team. Between the two rows, the little girl stands and sings *Oh Canada* to start the game.

The production was one of intense conflict. The Agency producer was self-serving and prone to dramatic exchanges. The Agency had agreed the shoot needed two, ten-hour days to complete the job. However, in the north, there are only five hours of useable sunlight each day. The Agency producer insisted the shoot should still be done in two days when it was obvious three were required. A Coke executive made her admit she was wrong. Embarassed, she chose to make the shoot difficult for everyone.

The director knew the story was on the edge of "too much." Nevertheless he was excited and engrossed in solving the problems of a new place with a local crew in minus-thirty-degree weather. Casting began in Vancouver where the hero was selected. Casting in Whitehorse was an evening on a local rink where the kids were eager to show their abilities.

None of the production people, director included, were properly prepared for minus thirty to fortydegree weather, so everyone was transported to the *Whitehorse Winter Clothing for Greenhorns Emporium* and each had their wallets thinned by about six hundred dollars. The long term advantage to this disadvantage was the number of Torontonians who have deep freeze winter wear stored in their basements, just in case.

Whitehorse had a community of workers who had a good mix of film and cold weather information. A previous shoot that had benefited from their skills was a car shoot that required a large and perfect ice surface on which to display their vehicles. The local crew invented a large cage on skates with ice-melting-flame-throwers mounted so they faced down. They were then towed back and forth across the lake, until the surface provided perfect reflections. The city did not yet provide a source for film equipment which meant the equipment for the shoot was trucked 2400 kilometres north from Vancouver. When the drivers arrived the day before the shoot following a harrowing trip, they were fed and hustled off to bed.

Because the rink for Coca-Cola was to be out on a lake and the actual surface was too rough to use, a man from the local crew drilled a hole in the ice, pumped up enough water to make a surface for a rink. The rink froze in an hour. The man then put large fans to work to blowing snow back onto the surface.

The local crew captain was an aboriginal gentleman who served as production manager. He also listed outdoor skills, writing and film direction on his business card. The crew rose early, and drove to the lake, well before sunrise. The temperature was minus thirty-nine degrees. Snow crunched and plumes of breath pushed from the many mouths. A heavy canvas tent went up first with a roaring wood stove and a warming room for children. Because the children's clothing had to look generic to the rest of Canada, warmth was produced with many layers. Pads warmed hands and feet but when shooting began, the average time a child could work in the open was only ten minutes. If discolouration occurred, the child was rushed into the warming room.

At the end, the crew agreed the cold weather gear was worth the money but had caused a problem in discerning who was who because everyone was dressed in the same outfit.

The footage was flown to Toronto and several versions cut. When the director saw the accepted commercial, he realized that he had failed to make a spot of the quality he had hoped. When the casting was done for the handsome hero, the director had not been happy with the selection but had been talked into accepting the choice. He gave in because the Agency said it didn't have the time or money to go further. The director should have picked a fight because although the young man looked like the right performer, his abilities as a performer were not mature enough to know how hard he had to work to convince his viewers the story was real. The director carries some of the blame for not being able to make the young man aware why his performance was missing the mark.

After the cut was approved in Toronto, in admiration for the efforts of the local kids, a Coke executive flew back to Whitehorse, rented a theatre and invited all the participants to the show. The kids enjoyed seeing themselves on film and the community recognized the generosity of the Coca-Cola Company.

Productions
&Executions

Conversations

Molson wanted a spot where a group of young fellows with the token chesty female friends built a raft for the summer cottage. For some forgotten reason, it had to be shot in California. Casting was an unusual experience in L.A. compared to the Canadian casting sessions of the time. There was a casting director, who conducted first interviews, and passed on a narrow segment of performers with appropriate abilities for the job. The selection was simple and chesty women were plentiful. The location manager found a lake in the mountains that had trees and ground cover similar enough to be mistaken for Ontario cottage country. After a check and client approvals, the production was a go. One of the young men was cast in Canada and when he arrived, the team loaded up and set out for the location.

The Canadian fellow ended up in the director's passenger seat and because the young man was humorous and interesting, a long conversation ensued. The subject of fame and varieties of success came up. He never expected to be a well known performer but he "enjoyed performing" and planned to continue in that occupation until his luck ran out. He asked if the director had ever worked with famous performers and the director launched into a long winded explanation of his inability to tolerate the pretensions that often accompanied people of note.

There was Leslie Nielsen on several locations for a Bank of Montreal shoot. Mr. Nielsen picked on a crew member who had a speech impediment on the Toronto location. At the Nova Scotia location, he acted out shamelessly at a birthday lunch, generously organized for him by the production company's producer. He got drunk and threw the cake. For the North West Territories location, he insisted the producer fly into Yellowknife ahead of him. That way, the attractive woman could meet him when he landed on the next flight and run across the concourse shouting, "Oh, Leslie, look, look, it's Leslie Nielsen."

Everyone present recognized Leslie as the brother of Eric Nielsen, a political force in the adjoining Yukon Territories. Leslie was pleased. Mr. Nielsen became a more reasonable human. "Ugly," commented the young man, "any others that yanked your chain?" "Lorne Green was a pain to work with, brusque and self-important. He made the mistake of leaving his wallet in his dressing room and was quick to blame everyone else for its disappearance. There was three hundred and fifty-four American dollars in the wallet and he didn't hesitate to insist the young producer replace exactly that amount from her ' purse. It was a Sunday before bank machines were invented.

Following this shoot, the director chose to avoid members of the 'star' community, finding it more comfortable to work with people who live in the real world and do not presume high status.

The charming young man told the director of one occasion when he was diminished and stated that "It doesn't happen very often and I can usually make a joke of it."

The sun came out at the right moment and an acceptable little spot was constructed from all the interesting moments that can be found while building a raft. The value of the young man was quickly apparent. He charmed his acting partners and kept things lively with his good humour.

Two young women in swim suits had promised they knew how handle a canoe. Cries from the lake proved otherwise. When asked what the difficulty was, the women confessed they didn't know how to canoe or swim and the breeze was refusing to let them return to land. That solved, a couple of beer close-ups and the shoot was finished. The early wrap gave everyone time for the long drive back to Los Angeles.

The director waved at his former passenger who was returning in an earlier car to catch a plane. He confided to the man standing beside him, "Charming guy, I think he'll do well, I keep forgetting his name." The man beside him answered the implied question.

"Martin Short"

Productions & Executions

Fake Lakes

It was apparently a moment critical to the advertisement of travel in and to Ontario and the provincial decision makers said "now." The production company jumped and a large stage was reserved for the project. The director enjoyed this kind of challenge and got out his drafting tools and scribbled furiously.

Shot #1 is a young man sitting on a rock in the middle of a pond, in front of a small waterfall and reading a book. The fit young man is accosted by his five year-old daughter who splashes him while he is trying to read. Shot#2 shows a young couple holding the opposite ends of a red cooler and stepping into the lake. They also have a small daughter, probably the same one but in a swim suit. Shot #2 is not shaded as shot #1 was; it is brightly lit with the sun's reflection on the water.

A member of the Ontario opposition party rose from his warm bed; had his toast and coffee then drove through a small blizzard to the legislature. He stood in the legislature and berated the government for spending money on lake construction when his province had so many beautiful lakes.

Both shots were accomplished with the same lake. Ontario paid $100,000 for the lake that was two lakes with a waterfall thrown in. Shot #1 was so well received, a frame from the film was enlarged and made into a billboard. The federal government paid millions to build a lake and justifiably bought a lot of negative flak.

Mr. Christie, who makes good cookies, decided to produce a writing contest and provide an annual reward for excellent children's books. The award was to be advertised in a commercial that showed as many adorable children as possible, all in the process of reading. Ideas were passed back and forth between Agency and director. A group was chosen with two

extra sequences attached in case one was weak. The only way to complete the shoot economically was to build 'frag sets' that facilitated movement from place to place. If an attempt was made to shoot the sequences on location, it would take about four days to shoot. The cost of set construction was high but was much less expensive than the cost of director and crew for extra days.

In studio, all of the sequences could be organized so they could be completed in one day. The studio situations held other advantages including the safety of the children and a range of lighting techniques.

The cinematographer on this memorable shoot was second to none. His patient manner facilitated speed and efficiency. The shoot that contained eleven situations was completed on time. The situations: 1. a child eating cookies under the kitchen table 2. a tiny boy incensed because his granddad fell asleep while reading him a story 3. a baby whose only clear word was "car" 4. a child sitting on the floor of the library reading a book 5. a mother reading to a new baby 6. a child reading a story to her stuffed animals 7. a child asleep in bed beside his book 8. a child sitting bare bummed on the toilet 9. a dad on the phone with a waiting child 10. a pretty girl with flowing blonde hair reading a story to her special needs brother who had spiky blonde hair 11. and finally a red headed kid reading a book while he sat on the end of a dock. Each situation was given a different atmosphere with different lighting and the shoot ended on time. The shot of the child on the dock was exquisite. Cedars leaned to a lake that existed only in the viewers imagination, cattails swayed a bit in the breeze, atmospheric perspective helped to make the moment real. A wash pan of water with broken mirrors lay below the boy's feet and produced a believable sparkle.

And then there was the shot of a tropical island needed immediately. The ocean ripple was created with plastic sheeting stretched across the studio in front of a painted island. The moment was captured on a long lens positioned outside the studio and across the street. Camera rolled intermittently between passing cars.

Productions &Executions

Before the Execution

Marketing is not normally seen as one of the exalted professions. Because of the reasonably recent appearance of the need to say *my product is better than yours,* advertising may not even be a profession. Professions are long established activities in which there is a mix of rational and emotional, cogent and belligerent activity.

At the time when the director worked as an art director for McKim Advertising, the advertising agencies met in an attempt to set a standard of behaviour. Somewhere in the midst of hand shakes and nodding heads, it was agreed the ugly practice of uninvited presentations to beer companies would be discontinued. Each of the Agencies returned to their glass and metal enclaves and told their creative departments that competition for beer advertising had been eliminated for all Agencies except themselves so 'get to work' on a new presentation right away. Creatives worked day, night and weekends, spies dispersed to find if the other Agencies were ahead of them or behind. Thousands of unremunerated hours went down the drain.

The primary competition was for a new beer called Red Cap. Vickers and Benson had a creative director named Terry O'Malley, a Rhodes Scholar / baseball fanatic / runner and writer. Mr. O'Malley didn't have his artists draw prodigious proposals. He hired a film crew and shot the commercial he wanted Molson to run for their new beer. V&B got the account. The commercial and concept were accepted and the Agencies that had exhausted their staff on failed presentations, knew they had shot themselves in their own private places. The V&B commercial embodied a new approach for local beer communications; it did not contain words, only a bunch of healthy young men in red caps on a golf course who raised their beer and their thumbs. No chesty women. Sales soared.

In the days before General Foods was purchased by Kraft, General Foods had the largest income producer in Jell-O and a valuable income producer in Maxwell House coffee. They never fooled with perfect Jell-O but were endlessly tweaking Maxwell House because of fluctuating public tastes. The product managers raised their arms in victory when research invented a system for vacuum-packing coffee. Those poor prairie people would finally be able to enjoy the taste of fresh coffee. Everyone was elated, huge profits were theirs to capture and the art director was given enough money to run a full page ad in western newspapers. The ad featured a steaming cup of coffee and a silver package that resembled a metal football. The metal football made a hissing sound when opened. Trains rolled west with the footballs and the product was given good facing on food chain shelves. The entire western population tried a sip and spat it on the ground. "Yuk!" they said, "Doesn't General Foods know what good coffee tastes like?" Westerners had been drinking stale coffee for so many years, they had become used to a stale coffee taste and wouldn't tolerate any other. Salesmen for General Foods were sent out the following week with pins. They punctured the hissing packs surreptitiously and allowed it to convert to a stale condition.

General Foods' next coffee invention was a freeze dried coffee named 'Maxim'. It lasted an even shorter length of time than the vacuum pack. When the public got their hands on it they said it was too strong so a plastic spoon with a half-bowl was attached to the package to help regulate the amount of coffee used. People frowned on plastic half spoons and sharp tasting coffee. General Foods lost another battle.

The next coffee for the public was presented with great flare and expense in a collectable apothecary jar. It appeared to be a flawless premium product well worth the extra money. They had the formula right, the taste was perfect and the product soared to unexpected heights. Suddenly, near the place General Food marketers called 'mature' or 'yellow light', a place where no product dies, sales of the product died overnight.

For a time, no reason seemed adequate for such
an unprecedented collapse. An investigation
ensued. It appeared that a new factor was an
active force in the world of marketing. Women
saved the pretty apothecary jars and once they
accumulated a nice group of them for the kitchen
window, they didn't want any more because their
moral sense did not allow them to throw out such
an attractive object.

The director has General Foods to thank for many
interesting projects and many generous paycheques.
He has always admired the appropriateness
of General Foods' marketing tool 'green light,
yellow light, red light'. General Foods' latest coffee
had just made a new speed record for arriving at
status Red. The product was dead.

While Molson has been as generous as General
Foods, the director is disappointed with the beer
companies' lack of courage. They are seemingly
unable to invent or trust a taste advantage. *Today
all beer advantages sit on the edge of imaginary.*
They have never accelerated their product
advantages beyond the suggestion that the
imbiber of their product will be more welcome in
the male community and much admired by their
sexual targets, if they drink the product. All of
which suggests they see their consumers as less
than sharp.

The director will take a run at this another time.

Productions &Executions

Adventure Tours

The landing at the Vancouver airport was bumpless (film talk) and free of drama. The crew gathered their tools in rental vans and headed northeast up the Trans Canada. At Hope, a left turn took them north. A bend in the gravel road revealed the town of Lillooet. Lillooet boasted an ancient and tiny log church above thirty modest homes. On the east side of town, a 'mechano set' bridge spanned the mighty Fraser. The director was in a rush to start his adventure. Unfortunately for him, soft vans were exchanged for metal box school busses and the team banged north then west for four hours on a road that occasionally came out of hiding to help the team on their way. The conclusion to the unfriendly ride was a long slope of warm sand that swept down to the river.

An adventure rafting company was on the shore and a short conference led by a member of the rafting company set safety standards and warned of the dangers of the river. The river apparently had a personality not to be tampered with and its personality changed each day. "Hah!" said the director. Rubber rafts were supplied with engines, equipment once again transferred. The expedition left mid-afternoon and gurgled south. At dinner, the lead raft landed on a sand bar and unloaded cooking tools and food. The evening was spent planning the techniques of the next day and whacking mosquitoes. Before sunrise and after a large breakfast of bacon, sand and eggs, the next leg was set to go. The plan was to access a visually exciting and adventurous piece of the Fraser River, where rafts bounce and tumble but no one dies. The camera crew rode the first raft that found rough spots. It was their job to land and set up camera to shoot the second raft as they rode by appearing and disappearing in deep troughs of water. The two rafts leap-frogged down the river. The canyon walls varied from vertical to expansive. Rafts almost rolled. No one was dry. In a place of narrow walls, the director's raft was swished into a bathtub the size of a back yard with an ugly whirlpool in the

centre. The driver pushed the engine to keep the raft clear of the hole; the raft rubbed a vertical wall and squeezed toward the exit. Just when everyone was sure they were safe, an entire thirty-foot tree shot straight up out of the water like an arrow and whacked down beside the raft. A look from the director and the driver shouted, "Trees and logs and whatever are pulled down where they stay for a very long time." The last part of the run-back down to Lillooet was more beautiful than exciting. The time allowed the director to regain his composure and make the decision whether or not the shots he had were adequate for the job.

A Bell helicopter skimmed the shores along the east coast of Newfoundland. The director had a seat with a magic window between his feet. Icebergs trundled along in a full range of sculptured shapes and variety of sizes. A berg off Bay Bulls had a fresh water lake on top.

Icebergs make Newfoundland a place of wonder. The commercial with an interest in icebergs was to be done for Molson. Probably their contention had something to do with beer ingredients but the director can't remember. Imagine, being paid for flipping around in a helicopter to shoot fantastic images of ice. We returned to Toronto, went to bed and in the morning there was a message from the producer we had employed in Newfoundland. A news article had appeared in the St. John's newspaper the day the team left Newfoundland. A large iceberg had pushed its way into the mouth of St. John's harbour. It sat trapped against the opening of the harbour while the push and roll of the ocean pounded the berg's bottom on an underwater rock. A man rowing across to St. John's, noticed signs the iceberg might break so he approached the berg with care. With a sound like a cannon shot, a huge chunk of ice broke and fell into the water. The remaining part lost its balance, rolling and twisting before it settled into a new position. The piece that had broken off shot back to the surface and snuggled up to its parent. The man in the dory was careful to solve the problem of the waves created by the berg, then continued on his way. As he passed the iceberg, he looked up and was amazed to see a Second World War bomber frozen in its face.

The numbers and identification were taken from the bomber and traced. It was established that the crew was not frozen in the iceberg but had been rescued. The aircraft, that was a part of Canada's contribution to the war effort, had run into mechanical difficulties and landed on the upward slope of a Greenland glacier.

The night after the iceberg split, it rolled again and the bomber was gone forever.

———————————

The director was aware this might be one of his last Molson adventures and was looking forward to the shoot. "The field is perfect," he said and walked off an area. "Build it here. I don't think we'll find a better spot."

In two days, the set builders put up the shell of a full sized barn and a side shed with an old truck tucked inside. The barn was uniquely constructed in that it was held in place with steel cables instead of wooden beams. In the middle of each span, a wooden block joined the two halves of the cable. Inside each block was an explosive charge. Electric wires ran from the blocks to a "piano" where the man in charge touched a key to separately ignite charges in their proper sequence. A safety cable was attached to the blind side of the barn. A vehicle hooked to the cable was there to ensure the barn went in the right direction. Before everyone was ready, the man in the vehicle thought he heard a "go" and began to pull the barn. Each of the five cameramen raced to cameras the assistants had already turned on. The director yelled "Do it!" The piano man strummed the charges. The barn came apart collapsing elegantly to the ground.

A baseball pitcher had been practicing his skills by throwing hardballs against the side of the barn. When he threw the perfect curve ball, the barn recognized his skill by collapsing in a cloud of dust.

The startled pitcher who no longer had a barn, sat down with a Molson.

Productions &Executions

Bottoms Up

A British bus is filled with a large number of noisy and happy passengers. They are on their way to a football (soccer) game. They sing and shout; they cheer for their team and have a wonderful time. The commercial for a British beer has twenty seconds of the passengers' glee and ten seconds where the camera pulls away from the bus and shows us it is pulling a beer truck. The brand of beer is clearly identified on the side of the truck and large pipes are seen joining the truck to the bus. The consumer is amused, appreciates the humour and remembers the name of the beer.

We are in a palace setting; the prince and the princess attempt to speak to the viewers of the commercial but their words are badly out of synch. Lip movements lead the words by half a second. A hand offers a tray with two Heineken beers. Prince and princess enjoy a sip of the beer and are, from that point on, appreciative and perfectly in synch.

The two European commercials are great examples of where the viewer is given pieces of an idea and enjoys the pieces enough to construct the product advantage for themselves. When consumers construct for themselves, the product advantage will not be forgotten.

Canadian beer advertising is boring. Why is beer's full potential for entertainment and information not accessed? Beer market managers are like artists who have used one brush for many years and are afraid to try another. Advertisers continue to construct beer ads that are more relevant to Viagra. Young people are loyal to a brand for a length of time so advertisers sell their base advantage to that segment. Governments asked the beer companies not to direct beer ads at young people but they continue to do so.

Beer advertising displays women as sexual candy and puts the wrong set to the minds of young viewers. I am surprised women continue to accept the diminishment. I'm surprised young men accept the suggestion their attraction mechanisms are underdeveloped and limited to the use of a mind-dulling substance. Market share is lusted after by marketers whose pay scale is often influenced by the share of the market they attract. Instead of a wide range of flavours appropriate to a wide range of uses, the marketers plod on, feeding a young public sexual attraction instead of providing them with a mind-extending range of product and product use.

———————

Beer has several qualities that can be used to sell itself: 1. a range of flavours appropriate for different foods 2. a style of beer with real advantages for a full range of consumers 3. beers for women 4. a beer of strengths and tastes relevant to specific needs. Creating useful beers would cause the marketer a lot of research and development dollars and would take a lot of the swing out of the rise and fall of temporary popularities. It would lower the high promotional costs that must accompany new brands. Over time, it would change the identification of beer preferences from emotional to intellectual, getting rid of implied promise and not believable advantage. Adults who don't drink beer because it is a dumb jock product, may come to appreciate the values of a beer brewed for a specific taste or a specific use. I'm embarrassed we don't engage in a smarter path and discover and use all the possible advantages of a product older than the wheel. The Research & Development door is open and we can escape from the dog days of beer. Take this blunt object off the shelves and give us products that still won't get us laid but will compliment our taste and intelligence.

I remember a visit to a monk's cavern deep in the Union of Soviet Socialist Republics about forty years ago. The film crew were invited to a lunch prepared in the manner of earlier times. They were given beef and potato stew with a large jug of potato beer that was unique and delicious. Bottoms up.

Productions & Executions

Miss Demeanor

The subject was rape and nobody had a cent to pay for the commercial. Would we mind doing it on our lunch hour with film ends, they asked? The Agency producer, for whom this was an important and private project, said, "Please don't tell my client" and introduced us to a young woman and a young man. Neither of the performers were members of the actors' union. The crew were members of one union, the cameraman and assistant were members of another and the studio was union controlled. The complete misdemeanour would amount to major trouble for all, if it was ever revealed. The director got everyone together, laid it out, explained the purpose of the project and was surprised when all the unionized people said rape was an important issue and gave it unanimous support.

The forty-five minute project began. The concept was that women could protect themselves better if they were not submissive in an attack. The fragile looking woman was a brown belt and beat the heck out of the young man for fifteen minutes (they were friends). The camera rolled throughout, at three and sometimes six frames per second. The result was a very small amount of film consumed and blurred images that gave a good impression of extreme violence.

The Agency producer was pleased. The crew were a geneous lot who had no complaints about the loss of lunch.

I can't remember what shoot it was, but there was a sudden ruffle of trouble in the clients' comfortable viewing area. Men stood, one looked under the television monitor and another was on his hands and knees under the table feeling the underside edges. A fearless female was shoving her hands down the cracks in the couch. The head honcho stood with hands on hips with a look of disgust on his face. The director was very curious as to what had happened so when he completed his shot, he walked over and asked what the fuss was about.

The Agency producer (a male this time around) explained that an accusation had been made by the client that there was a hidden microphone in the client area that transferred the client's and Agency's comments to the director. Apparently, each time someone made a comment about a shot shown on the monitor, the director, who was about thirty feet away on the shooting floor, spoke to someone and corrected the problem.

The director smiled and said he would help in the search but to his knowledge a microphone did not exist. He explained the phenomena occurred because he was looking at the same shot on another monitor and discovering the same flaws at the same time as the people in the client enclave. "Just yell if I miss one," he said.

Productions &Executions

Miss Adventure

It was both an interesting and truly boring shoot. The interesting part was that the shoot included Canmore, Honolulu, Texas, Segovia in Spain, Zagreb, Yugoslavia and Innes, Ireland and they promised to pay a director for travelling to all those places. The boring part? A very brief and similar shot was to be taken in each place. The end product was a commercial introducing a new credit card and the financial institution wanted everyone to know the card could be used in a multitude of places. At each, easily identifiable location, a performer would look into the camera and tell the audience the card was used where he or she lived.

The crew was off and running the day after the job was introduced because everyone was in a hurry. *The plan.* The airplane would get the crew to the region before noon. On arrival the team split, director and cameraman looked for locations, producer and client interviewed performers. In the afternoon and perhaps into the evening, camera rolled on a sequence. The next morning the team caught an airplane to the next part of the world. Occasionally the system did not work e.g. the flight from Texas to Madrid left on a Texas morning and arrived in a Spanish evening. Glitches were overcome at each location but all concurred the system did the job. The shoot ended on time.

Inside the first layer of Rocky Mountains, on the Rafter Six Ranch that straddles the Kananaskis River, there was an iconic horse corral. The performer in the cowboy hat sat on the top rail and proclaimed the client's credit card useful in western Canada. In Segovia, a Spanish gentleman stood in the armoury of an ancient and spectacular castle just down the road from a three-storied Roman aquaduct and delivered a speech similar to the cowboy's. A street vendor in Zagreb proclaimed his city ready for transactions with the new card. In Honolulu, a grass hut was required so the director and cameraman went searching.

Soon it was apparent that no one in modern day Honolulu lived in a grass hut. About two in the morning, on a road south of Honolulu, the car lights swept a sign on a wire fence that contained an illustration of a grass hut. In the process of climbing the fence, the cameraman muttered, "Sign says zoo." They were too tired for the idea to properly register and they advanced through the trees to an open area. The grassy clearing was covered with what appeared to be tree stumps. Then the tree stumps moved. The director and cameraman raced for the fence, clearing it quickly but leaving pieces of clothing attached to the barbs on top. While escaping, the two men had glimpsed the perfect location, a perfect grass hut, with a perfect overhanging palm, in front of a body of water with an island arranged behind. The zoo manager was aroused from a sound sleep, the hotel restaurant staff held over, gates unlocked and animals secured.

As the sun broke the horizon, a generous and attractive woman sat at the door of the grass hut at the end of a delicious luau. There had been a rising ambient sound and as she opened her mouth to speak, the air was filled with the deafening thunder of military jets roaring off the island and clearing the grass hut by about fifty feet. The director and cameraman had chosen an idyllic spot at the end of a runway. It was agreed by sign language that the woman would mouth the required message and the words would be dubbed afterwards.

The Innes location was a crossroad at the white-washed and stone-walled centre of the village. The performers were three, tow-haired boys and a man from a popular Irish television show. Everything was set for a shot where the boys played soccer and the performer would step in and display his soccer skills. The performer was not perfectly prompt. Finally, his car pulled up and the performer stepped out. It seemed every door in the village flew open and the town rushed forward. They grabbed the performer and rushed him into the bar at the crossroad. When the townspeople had finished with their famed performer, his knees no longer functioned and his slackened tongue turned words into unidentifiable sounds. The shot was rescheduled for the next day. With constabulary protection and some crowd control, the townspeople allowed the performer to do his job.

Shaw had become a big name in television and a commercial was required for their B.C. viewers. The concept was acceptable. A little boy was eager to help his parents set up the Christmas dinner table and the little fellow wobbled back and forth carrying fragile objects. The parents were having a pleasant time in the kitchen and didn't find out until the last moment that the little boy and his sister had set up dinner in the den, instead of the dining room. In the den, a light table draped in an oversize tablecloth, was pushed against the television set so they could have Christmas dinner with their absent grandmother via a recently introduced Shaw system.

The crew rolled camera even though the Shaw overseer had not yet arrived. They were close to finishing the kitchen sequence when the Shaw rep appeared. She walked onto the set, took a fleeting look at the kitchen and said "I don't like it, I want something Ikea." Everything that did not involve the kitchen was shot through the remainder of that day and the crew wrapped early. Overnight, a new kitchen was constructed and the team worked through the second day to shoot the kitchen for a second time. At lunch, the Shaw person declared that at the conclusion of the shoot, the Ikea kitchen was to be sent to her home in Calgary and everyone understood why they had been delayed. The shoot finished later than everyone wanted, with the children confused and the crew with a bad taste in their mouths. The director returned to his hotel miffed because an efficient use of time was a point of pride. The Shaw person returned to her Calgary home to await her new kitchen. Shortly after the installation of the new kitchen, she was asked to look for another job.

Miss Takes

The ball-like object that is attached to bumpers for pulling trailers looked like it would do the job. The muscular Dodge truck backed into place and the hitch and a shackle were firmly attached. A hemp rope about two inches thick was tied to the shackle and the other end of the rope attached to a large bulldozer with its huge blade stuck in the ground. The idea was that Dodge trucks were tough and this truck was about to prove its toughness by yanking at the rope and raising the wall of a barn. The director's intention was to first show the rope snapping to a taut line and then cut to the wall of the barn rising.

The truck was prepared, the rope coiled so it would not tangle and the cameraman set up his machine, four feet in front of the dozer and six inches from the rope. When everything was in place, the cameraman bent to put his eye to the camera, the truck raced its engine and the director was suddenly hit by the idea of an impending calamity. He saw it so clearly, his good friend and skilled workmate was about to die. "Whoa!" he yelled. After a loud and lengthy argument between friends, the director refused to continue the shot unless the cameraman stood at a safe distance from the camera. The cameraman eventually consented to move his body twenty-four inches to the right. The camera, with eyepiece covered in a cloth, rolled. The truck spun its tires and the rope leapt from its coiled stance and became a line drawn with a ruler. The rope did not break; it stretched like a huge rubber band. It still did not break, the shackle hung on to the hitch. The hitch was strong and did not break. The culprit was the bumper. The bolt that held the ball pulled through the bumper like a knife through butter. The ball and the hitch became missiles that snapped back, missed the camera by a hair and put a one-inch dent in the solid steel dozer blade. When the missile had finished the dent in the dozer, it looked for the cameraman, smacked him in the leg and knocked him to the ground. After a trip to the hospital, and a two hour delay, the cameraman returned to the shoot. For all who asked, he pulled up his pant leg to display a bruise that was a perfect and bloody imprint of the car keys that had been in his pocket.

When the footage was examined, the part that fascinated everyone was seeing that the returning shackle and ball were visible in only two film frames. A camera runs at twenty-four frames per second. The missile returned one hundred feet to the dozer blade, in one-twelfth of a second.

Miss Direction

The skeleton of the barn was a number of large beams that were saved on the property of a man who made log structures near Tweed, Ontario. The beams were used many times for a variety of film needs and consistently created interesting rustic structures.

An insurance company needed a barn interior. It was the middle of winter so a portion of the Tweed barn was put up in a studio. The commercial featured a small boy sitting on a box beside a wood stove, listening to his aboriginal grandfather tell him stories. The grandfather was very elderly and fragile and a medical person was present to keep an eye on his condition at all times. Lunch time arrived and the aboriginal gentleman approached the director. "I know you are a storyteller, I am the storyteller for the people of my community. Would you permit me to tell a story at the conclusion of lunch?" The director agreed and when lunch was over, the grandfather stood and told the story of a British Columbia tribe who knew how man had come to live on earth.

According to the tribe's verbal records, a small bear who lived in mountains that fringe the Pacific, was continually terrified by larger bears. One day, the small bear was tracking down a marmot for his lunch, when he spotted the approach of a very large bear. He was so frightened he hid in a cave and took off all his fur. When he stepped out into the open, the big bear did not recognize him as a bear and walked right on by. In this way, humans first appeared on earth. The storytelling ate into the crew's shooting time but the director was not concerned because the shoot was simple. He completed his shots by three o'clock and after a half-hour clean-up, everyone went home.

It was pointed out to the director that some Agency producers just like to be on budget, while some see their job as milking a full day's work from director and crew. There are even a few Agency producers who insist on sixteen-hour shoots and wrongly see themselves as getting two eight-hour days for the price of one.

In his first days in a studio, the director wasn't looking for a position with a label; he just had a large curiousity and wanted to learn more about film. How it was exposed, how it cut and what exactly were the aesthetics of movement? An incident that took place in his art school days had given him a secure stance in graphic art. An assignment had been handed in late, a five percent per day penalty was promised. The assignment came back with a red, clear, one hundred percent marked at the top. When the art instructor was asked why he did not impose the penalty, he explained, "I am the president of the school; I get to put whatever mark I choose on the assignment." The incident wiped away any doubts the director had about his ability to make good visual decisions.

He was confident he could find his way in film. He was good at dirty work when it was required. He buckled down to gather the pieces of the puzzle. He swept the studio, took out the garbage and ran multiple errands for several months and stepped into ad agencies' views when he completed a couple of attractive still life moments. A small agency gave him a small job and in the process someone referred to him as a director. To this day, the director sees the title of *labourer in the design of visual communications* as a more suitable title.

Feature directors are people with aggressive instincts and artistic experience who have a vision for the construction of a story. When they put it on film, they have control of the aesthetic and emotional rendition of the story. A commercial director seldom has control. She or he has an art director and a writer close by and a marketing team less than fifty feet away. Everything a commercial director does is second-guessed before the director says "cut." The director is not a person who renders a personal vision. The director is a superbly paid member of a team that renders the vision of the team. The director is a marketing straw boss, in charge of rendering. Ridley Scott and Bronwyn Hughes are examples of commercial directors who became feature directors. They had to learn new skills before they could make the transition.

Sometimes a famous film director is awkward as a commercial straw boss.

Ontario Hydro hadn't spent enough of the public's money on generation so they decided they needed a couple of commercials. An orientation meeting was called. Production house, Agency president and 'Hydro Person of Considerable Importance' were to be in attendance.
The Agency president arrived early and told the director and the meeting that he would be turning the meeting over to the director for a description of the shoot. He then asked for assurance the director would describe A, B, and C in "this way." The director agreed, the meeting ensued and the director described A, B, and C in the manner he had promised. The Person of Importance blew his top and said that he would not allow A, B and C to be done that way in his commercial. How could he be so foolish to consider such an unreasonable execution of A, B and C?
The Agency president, showing the same level of anger, turned to and demanded of the director why he had chosen such a foolish direction of A, B and C? The director did his best to stumble backwards and assume the responsibility for his foolish blunder. Engulfed in his own anger, he spent the next hours wondering at the weak-kneed performance of the Agency president and how he had seen other men handle similar situations with greater intelligence and courage.

The following evening while deep in sleep, the director's pituitary gland quit and he was rushed to the nearest hospital. The vacancy created by the director's departure, was eventually filled by David Cronenberg. Mr. Cronenberg, after his successful feature experiences, had been looking forward to attempting a run at 'straw boss'. He was surprised at how little time he was given to create the moments agreed upon.

The editor assigned to do the cut was troubled by takes that were not shot in a manner that easily accommodated a thirty-second length.

Moving into either discipline is a learning opportunity.

Commercial directors who expect to have freedom from suggestions and critique, end up doing something else for a living. However, the art director, who rides the director's ear, will not shoot with that director very many times. The same is true of the Agency creative director who comes up with a brand new idea in the middle of a shoot. When he does that, he erases the extra shots the director was trying to find time to do for him.

Producers, directors, Agency or production house people of whatever catagory, who have an agenda other than the success of the job, are seen as bottom feeders and are avoided.

In the thirty-five years the director has worked in the commercial world, he remembers only six jobs that were run with minimum or no supervision. The six jobs produced two gold Bessies and two awards of merit. The director recommends Agencies do their research and hire directors they trust.

Productions &Executions

Short Ends & Leftovers

When the fragile, precious heritage Kraft wagon came racing over the hill at full gallop with the driver riding the wagon tongue and the horse's ear in his teeth, it was a critical moment for the director and a sad moment for the fellow who was so proud of the wagon.

Proud of his knowledge of his home province, he confidently turned the bend and entered Horse Thief Canyon. He was north of Drumheller with his important client in the back and his favourite untouched valley ahead. What greeted his eyes was a fifteen-house village in his valley that hadn't been there two weeks ago. A crew for the movie Superman had snuck in ahead of him.

It took five hours to harness the six Belgian horses that pulled the thundering beer wagon down a cobblestone street in Old Montreal. Finally, the driver made a clicking sound to signal the horses and the mighty vehicle rolled forward into the street. For a while all was well but as the cobble-stones got a little rougher, all the glass and agate decorations began to fall from the harness and were soon crushed under mighty Belgian feet.

In tidy Leaside, when the rain-bar was raised above the house at three o'clock in the morning, the director turned to the crew and jokingly requested, "Let there be rain." When the rain-bar refused to send down any water, an investigation discovered the hydrant water in Leaside did not have enough pressure to make rain or fight a fire over twelve feet high. The director lost his shot for that night but gifted the town with the knowledge that any building over twelve feet high would burn to the ground unless they fixed the pipes.

The director finally found the perfect house for his shoot in the north end of the Mount Pleasant area of Toronto. A local and disapproving lawyer went door to door with a petition demanding those awful film people be banished. The director was upset.

He was less upset when he learned a competitive production company, working in the area, was known to have punched a hole in the wall of a private home to facilitate a long lens.

An enthusiastic storm shut down a Newfoundland shoot. The director and cameraman had seen all the tourist sites on other shoots so they had nothing to do. They got together, played chess and at each mealtime, 'ate the menu', starting with the top line and at the next mealtime, after several more games, they ate the second line and so on for as many days as the storm lasted.

In the end, the storm had lasted just the right length of time. The Newfoundland Hotel had a better than average chef and the director's ego could not stand the loss of any more games.

The shoot resumed.

At twenty below on a ski hill somewhere in Ontario, the director was asked to shoot a Skidoo coming down the ski hill. The commercial made the claim that Skidoo was a tough and reliable machine to use for safety patrols on ski hills. Ski patrols were made at dusk to ensure no one in difficulty was left on the hill. To suit the concept, the headlight of a shiny new machine was to clear the crest of the hill in the opening seconds, and without pause, travel to the bottom in exactly fifty-seven seconds. At the bottom it would pass the camera and display its perfect self for three seconds, before the sixty-second spot ended.

The test run in daylight showed that unless the machine traveled at a ridiculous speed, the run could not be accomplished in less than three minutes. The writer was distraught. Someone had an idea that took us to dusk to work out. The idea allowed the run to have two unseen minutes over the time limit. When later cut to twenty-seven seconds, it appeared to be a continuous run. When dark arrived, the camera rolled, the Skidoo popped over the crest of the first hill and camera followed, as it moved down to a point where it disappeared. When it disappeared, the camera stopped and was locked in position. The Skidoo travelled unseen, to a point on the top of the next hill, that was lined up with the point where it had disappeared. Camera focused on that point and rolled as the Skidoo was seen to travel down the second section. When it disappeared, it was again moved to a point where it would reappear, aligned to the point where it had disappeared. The trick was continued until the machine was on its last run and had to accelerate to make the run on time. Two minutes of travel were eliminated by two large moves and one short one.

The writer was happy; he ran his unending monologue beside an unending Skidoo run.

Productions &Executions

Great Expectations

Somewhere north of Toronto, about the height of King City, resting against a suburban village, an ancient cut in the land provides film crews with beautiful places to shoot.

The creek tumbles past the rugged remains of an early grist mill. The fall of water, that the mill once used, has carved a rococo array of bathtubs from the soft stone. The bathtubs give their contents to a small lake with an island in the middle. The lake squeezes the water through a canyon into a marsh and the marsh opens to a good sized lake.

The director's first shoot that accessed the visual values of the canyon was about a fisherman in a small boat who caught a fish so big it pulled his boat around in circles. His friend, who was sitting in a chair on the dock, saw his friend rotating in circles, stood up and his chair toppled into the water. When he went to sit back in his chair, he found there was no longer a chair and followed his chair into the lake. It was an interesting technical problem and on the pre-shoot location check, everyone worked on how this little drama was to be constructed. It was decided a boat was to be given attachments that would allow it to rotate on the spot. A cable would run underwater to the boat, from the island, to hold it in place. Another cable would be wound around a large spool under the boat. When the cable was pulled from the shore, the pull on the spool would rotate the boat. The fisherman's line would be attached to a wooden appendage on the spool and its position would give the appearance of pulling the boat in circles. "Very good," agreed everyone and dispersed to start the necessary tasks. Before the shoot, someone asked the question, "Do you want to do this more than once?" A properties man, with scuba abilities, was added to the crew so the spool could be rewound in the water for take two.

The day came and everything was in place. What ensued is a reminder that directors should always expect the unexpected. TAKE #1 The boat rotated in circles but when the fisherman pulled on his line and leaned backwards, he tipped the boat enough to bring the spool's appendage up out of the water. TAKE #2 The cable tangled and produced only half a turn. TAKE #3 Waiting for the rewind was taking too long, and a crew member started to wade in to see what was wrong. The scuba properties man popped up breathing hard; he had become tangled in the cable. The rotation was slow but could be speeded up in post. TAKE #4 The rotation worked perfectly in brown water. The flailing of the trapped scuba diver had stirred the soft bottom of the lake.

A year or so later, the director recommended the lake at the bottom of the canyon for a shoot for Boy Scouts of Canada. The Idea of the shoot was to make a summer at Boy Scout camp look like an interesting thing to do. Casting was easy. The troops were eager.

A tight shot down the creek showed the arriving campers as they pulled into the lake. They tipped their canoes and fell, laughing, into the tepid water. A wide, establishing shot made the lake look like a nice place to swim. The kids were good looking and healthy and there was something attractive in every shot. A group of young people started to fool around on the swimming raft. It turned into a competition to see who could do the most ridiculous exit from the raft. The director didn't direct, he just rolled the camera, the kids were doing a good job directing themselves. After lunch, a few more shots and a comfortable shoot began to wrap.

Everyone's attention shifted to a young man who didn't want to leave the water. He had been the hero of the raft's improvised contest. He jumped higher, farther and with more abandon than all the other boys. He was handsome and the girls all thought him attractive. The father of one of the younger kids was concerned for him. He walked into the lake to ask the boy why he didn't want to come out when everyone else was leaving. The father returned with a smile on his face and felt around in his duffle bag.

"He's lost his trunks."

Productions & Executions

"If you can think and not make thoughts your aim."

Rudyard Kipling

In the director's opinion, based on forty years of working on communicating concepts, we are weaker than we used to be. Too many commercials do not earn adequate interest or response, *i.e. do their job.*

They seem to be written for the advancement of a writer and shot for the advancement of a director rather than a product. A downturn in the industry became obvious when American Agencies were given permission to buy Canadian Agencies. The change in the regulations worked well for Americans. It also worked well for Canadian Agency owners who saw an opportunity to get their money out. It was not a 'win, win' situation. It was a 'win, win, lose' situation. Fewer commercials were made in Canada, more American commercials, with minor adjustments, were run in Canada because of lower cost. Production companies were stung. Large creative departments were replaced by smaller ones. The director sees these cutbacks as a part of the reason for the decrease in conceptual marksmanship. Agency executives, who hire young and consequently cheaper creatives, incorrectly dress themselves in the idea that an inexperienced creative is as effective as an experienced one.

Another principal flaw is a gap in the education of Agency executives. If Agency executives learned to recognize creative work that did not hit their identified target, they would be better appreciated by the client who contracted them. Political powers within an Agency often intimidate an executive and make it impossible for them to turn down a proposed execution. The executive, who is face-to-face responsible to the client, must have the power to stop the team and re-shoe the horses. If executives agreed with creative directors on a standard of effective communication, the new creative who placed his needs ahead of his client's, would have to walk a finer line.

The Canadian agency who handled the transition best was Vickers and Benson, run by Terry O'Malley. Mr. O'Malley had strong influence over both the executive and creative levels and enjoyed the personal contact with his clients.

In 1965, a senior account executive named Mickey Fair did not accept his creative director's contention that a concept for Canada's first Banking campaign needed refining. He defied the C.D. and presented the campaign to the head of the bank. The campaign ran, won top awards, and was copied by other banks throughout the United States. The creative director, who had demanded the idea be put on pause, wrote a nice apology.

A destructive impression that runs through many Agencies is the idea that creativity is an exclusive tool belonging only to members of a department designated "creative." If executives of all categories believed in their own ability to select a good execution, the creative department would have to sharpen their tools. Creatives have to recognize their companion departments as equally creative. A woman in Media, when asked for a schedule for the distribution of a photo ad for newspaper replied, "Why are we shooting an expensive shot when we know the address of every person we want to contact?" Every member of an Agency should be confident in their own judgement and be free to make their opinions known. They should also be reminded that no one has ever brought forward an advertising idea that is anything more than something interestingly constructed from used parts. Agencies will work better when their 'creative' departments are called 'invention' departments. Perhaps creatives would then be required to have a university degree. We could leave the word 'creative' for social elevation applications. 'Creative' always arrives at the party over-dressed, manoeuvres for position and builds an unjustified wall.

The director taught a group of college students and they came up with a solution to this problem. They concluded humans have a physical feature that certifies their creative ability - a belly button.

We can make our communications more effective. Viewers are tiring of us, invention is a tool not a toy.

The abilities of good communication were first demonstrated to the director when he looked up at a billboard in New York City. The billboard did not have an image, just the words,

"I QUIT SCHOOL WHEN I WERE 16"

A Toronto bus carried an advertisment across the back that read,

"WOULD THE MAN WHO TOOK THE NISSAN FOR A TEST DRIVE LAST THURSDAY, PLEASE RETURN IT."

A newspaper ad carried a large picture of a rough looking black man, then listed a series of brutal acts. The ad ended with the statement, "The accused is not shown here, the photo is of the detective who arrested the accused." In all three cases, the ads provide viewers with enough information to be able to devise their own answers.

Viewers remember messages they have given themselves better than any message we can concoct for them.

The director was in New York because he was the newest and the most expendable member of McKim's creative department. The convention on the subject of "Creativity" was for his edification and an opportunity to drag home pieces of information for other members of his department. Top creative writers and art directors from the better known Agencies, were making interesting speeches. A famous creative spoke of the illness called "I" disease and claimed it was common to most Agencies. An interesting writer spoke under the banner "Memorability" and stood without speaking until the room was empty. A man who made a failing car dealer famous by staging a medieval joust between a car from the dealer and an armoured knight on a white horse, spoke eloquently of a *skill* called *creativity* that we all have the ability to access.

Productions &Executions

Difference & Dissention

A quiet, intelligent and relatively inexperienced advertising executive was hired by a large, able and publicly owned Agency. After a year or two, he let it be known he had purchased a number of shares in the company and would like to have the responsibility of re-routing and re-organizing the mechanics of the corporation. Long-time executives were insulted and incensed; sides were taken, financial weapons drawn. The creative director took the opposing side to the new employee. The company was split fifty-fifty.

The new employee waited until he had accumulated fifty-one percent of the shares of the company and announced he was now CEO of the Agency. The creative director, who had opposed the CEO's rise to power, was given the choice of leaving or being given a tiny appendage office.

Small branch offices are a common Agency device that give the Agency a dumping ground for accounts they no longer need or that stand in the way of attracting larger accounts. For a time, the mother Agency prospered under its new CEO. When the value of the Agency had increased in value, it was suddenly sold. The tiny appendage struggled to survive. Its president attempted to raise his Agency out of miniature into middle importance by displaying its creative ability. Without consulting his staff, he hired a New York production house to build a blimp, put the name of a pipe tobacco company on its side and shot it as it lifted from the Scarborough bluffs. The tobacco company did not see this as an advertisement that fit its image and refused to run it. The appendage crumbled.

In an unrelated incident and some years later, the marketing manager for Canada Saving Bonds sent a film crew to Salmon Cove on the east coast of Newfoundland. The storyboard showed two female friends having a wonderful reunion as they walked around the cove.

Their meeting was casual, one was dressed in her work clothes and the other in the clothes she wore for her visit home. The two performers chosen to portray the friends, liked each other on sight and although they did not share a common background, they found many things to talk about as they wandered from place to place. The director could have gone home; the women produced their own completely natural and undirected moments. On the grassy top of the cliffs that edged the cove, the director carefully covered the shots he had promised. A close-up of the children who had joined the two women, allowed the ladies to relax for a moment. When the director turned around to re-engage them, he found them lying on their backs in the grass, legs in the air mimicking dance steps they had known as young women. Recognizing the value of the moment the director positioned them so the cove was in the background and shot the upside down dance for the commercial. The moment confirmed once more, the practice of booking performers on the basis of their personality, rather than on the basis of their appearance. The director has been gifted with many more interesting takes than the ones he devised.

The town of Salmon Cove was generous with the film crew; residents lent a hand and offered opinions on locations. Many came to watch the unusual but boring process. When the producer asked for permission to enter a property, he was introduced to a young lady with Down Syndrome. The person making the introduction added the comment that the young lady didn't get out much. The producer invited the young lady to come and watch the shoot which she did and enjoyed very much. After the shoot, a resident of position invited the crew to his home on the hill, and generously entertained them and filled them with the best of the local cuisine.

The Salmon Cove, Canada Saving Bond commercial ran once. An associate of the marketing manager saw it and remarked to the manager, "I didn't know you were in favour of gay relationships." The easily frightened manager put the commercial in a bottom drawer and didn't take it out until a few words of clarification were added to the script.

Productions &Executions

Greeks & Gifts

The casting community said there were very few Greek performers in the country, let alone fifteen in Toronto. McCain had invented a Greek pizza after inventing many others pizzas with an ethnic bent and wanted to run a commercial with enthusiastic Greek people enjoying their new pizza. The commercial was to include a robust gathering of about fifteen people. The camera would slide into the gathering and collect shots of happy people enjoying the McCain product. A dance would ensue and a grandfather and a young man would be featured in a characteristically Greek dance. All this sounded acceptable except for lack of enough authentic Greeks.

The director asked his casting director Jeff Marshall, what he could do. The man's shoulders slumped and he shuffled off with a minimum of enthusiasm. Two days later he was on the street in an area where Canadians of Greek heritage lived and shopped, pulling anyone who looked the least bit Greek off the street. With his enthusiasm renewed and his natural charm engaged, he got a group of locals to go through the community and find everyone who had ever thought of performing. By the shoot day, he had a thorough array of Greek performers and the production was off and running.

McCain's had hoped the party could be shot in a location that appeared to be Greek but the location hunters just couldn't find a white stone house on a cobblestone street in T.O. A tiny piece of Greece was constructed in a Toronto studio. The cinematographer made the sunlight sparkle down through the trees that were not there and all the people who had never been to Greece said it sure looked like Greece to them. Jokes aside, the set builder did a good enough job that a viewer phoned the TV station when the spot was put on the air and claimed he knew where the spot had been shot, just down the street from his mother's house in Greece.

The McCain story reminded the director of the many times the abilities and enthusiasm of the people he worked with had made him look like he knew what he was doing. Film people come from everywhere and are filled with the challenge of their work. They have systems and patterns, inventions and as many personalities as there are people. The director's crew was willing to support him because he brought them business. They were continually helpful, all the way to the point where on a particularly rough day, a crew member said quietly, "If you want to stay in the business, you would be wise to lose the temper."

John Davidson was raised in Scotland and came to Canada as a master carpenter. His first job in Canada was to install the wooden pegged hardwood floors in E.P. Taylor's mansion. The director got to know and admire John as the gregarious key grip on most of his shoots.

On a night when the crew was resting in an aging motel north of Huntsville, the director was crossing the parking lot when he noticed he was being accompanied by a huge toad. He picked it up, took it to John's room, where all the boys were drinking their evening allotment. In order to cool down from the day's exertions, John was always naked on his bed in these situations. The director carefully placed the huge toad on John's generous belly and told him he figured he had found one of his relatives. A race ensued in which a completely naked John didn't give up until a car pulled in off the highway and swept the parking lot with headlights. The director paid the price the following day.

A few days before he retired, John went missing. His concerned friends finally found him in his boat where he had attempted some plumbing repairs behind the toilet. John had been thoroughly stuck in a tight place for two days. When the director asked him what he was going to do during his retirement, he replied, "First, I'm going to find a home in Scotland beside a golf course. Second, I will collect apprentice plans that are drawn as a final test by graduating carpenters in my home town."

He did.

John was loved by all his working partners including
the novice director he helped to build.

The director had a house he was building over
one hundred miles from Toronto.
He had the roof half shingled.
The forecast called for an early snow.

The next morning he awoke to find his crew chief
John Sheridan and the crew parked in his driveway.

The director recognizes that he owes the people he worked with,
grips and gaffers, properties people and continuity policemen,
producer persons and many others,
a debt of thanks and friendship.

Productions & Executions

What's yer Beef.

When the director heard that a chain of American restaurants named Black Angus wanted him to do some commercials, he was intrigued. The director's mother, still articulate in her nineties, told him the story about Black Angus that follows.

In central Alberta where she lived in her teens, the most popular beef cattle were the white faced Hereford. A group of seven gregarious brothers, who had lots of cattle of their own, enjoyed borrowing and re-branding their neighbour's cattle. It was lots of fun, very easy to cut three strands of wire and ten 'white face' were hardly missed. When a man named Arthur found the repaired hole in his fence he knew who the villains were and he recognized that he had a problem much larger than the missing cattle.

The valley in which this all took place was a tight and happy community. The seven brothers sat beside Arthur's family in the only church. The wives of the seven brothers were close to all the other wives. The kids from both families went to the same school. The wives had a rug-making club called the *Happy Hookers*. If Arthur caused a stink about ten cows, he was going to destroy his community. He thought about it for a while, collected ten nickels, boiled them, cut a tiny slit in the shoulder of ten cows and put a nickel in each slit. He put the ten cows in the pasture with the repaired fence and waited. When the cows went missing, he called in the R.C.M.P., told them the story, and they ambled over to the ranch owned by the seven brothers.

At the brothers' denial, he dismounted and showed the officer the nickels in several newly branded shoulders. The officer began to read the brothers their rights when Arthur said "Whoa, constable, I don't want them charged. I want them to buy all my cattle." Arthur had ten thousand acres so that was a lot of cows. 'Broke' was better than 'busted'. The brothers coughed up the money for all of Arthur's white-faced cattle.

Arthur went off to Red Deer and bought the very best pure-bred Black Angus available. No one was told what had taken place, none of Arthur's cows were ever stolen again and the community rolled happily along.

The American chain named Black Angus was shocked. A competitor had put out an excellent commercial, in which a crayon-drawn chicken urged customers to enjoy their delicious beef dinner and a crayon-drawn cow urged customers to buy only their fabulous chicken. Black Angus wanted a tongue-in-cheek tough cowboy to remind the public that Black Angus was the best beef there was. They wanted a commercial shot beside a creek in the dry Arizona bush and one shot in heavy snow in Montana high country. They had brought their business to Canada because Canadian dollars were close to half the value of American dollars, i.e. If they used Canadian, they got two commercials for the price of one.

The director's accomplished set builders constructed early morning Arizona in one part of the studio and high country snow in another and the production company shot the two commercials. The company was sure two successful commercials and gifts of Canadian maple syrup would bring Black Angus back soon. The next commercial they sent north was a cowboy shaving in an ice filled creek in the dead of winter. The director made the mistake of telling them they had a perfect location for that at Steamboat Springs, Colorado.

And the idiot said this when the two countries' dollars were almost par.

Productions & Executions
Exit Stages

It was the third time the director had opened the gate to retirement. He had a few things to do before retreating to some kinder interests and tried to do a good job for Bell before he packed his bags. He didn't tell Bell it was his last job because he had already had two other 'last shoots'. Bell liked the outcome of the Christmas commercial with the boy on the school bus and they gave him a try at three Telecommunication spots. Their message was about the way our lives could be improved with Bell service. The spots were well written and held the promise they would be interesting to shoot.

The first spot was about a truck driver who bettered himself by taking courses from an online university.

The second was a young woman doctor whose office was in an industrial trailer in the far north. In order to confirm her diagnosis, she used face to face contact with Toronto specialists over the internet. The patient was a five-year-old boy, who sat on an examination table in front of the far away specialists and looked very brave.

The third was the story of a man in a remote cabin who liked to order pizza from people who guaranteed the arrival time of the pizza. He was so remote, the pizza he got was always free and very cold. The location chosen for the remote cabin was an island in Georgian Bay about fifteen kilometres from Honey Harbour and half a kilometre from the shore. It looked like a very lonely spot.

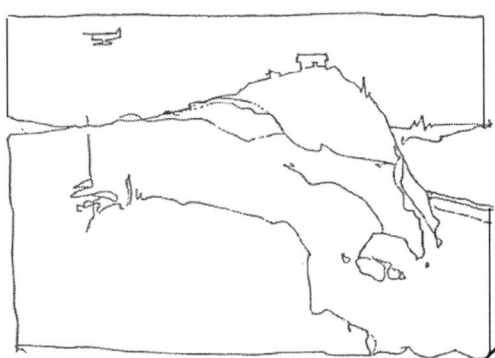

There wasn't a cabin on the tiny island, just a bush and two tiny trees. The director's amazing construction crew put half a cabin in place in two days. There was only a half cabin because the interior of the cabin had already been shot in a Toronto studio and the cabin on the island would only be filmed from the shore side. The story was changed a little from the writer's conception because all felt the loneliness was better underlined by surrounding water than surrounding bush. For the wide shot, a boat struggled to shore with imaginary supplies.

The locals showed their good humour when they asked the crew not to dismantle the cabin. Their explanation? A person, who owned the cottage directly behind the island, visited for two weeks every year and was a loud and abrasive pain in the bottom. This person incorrectly claimed the island as his. Rather than listen to his annual eruption, they had finally found a way to shut him up. He would assume the mock-up cabin on HIS island was a new cottage and they would all gather round to enjoy the fireworks that would surely follow.

In going over the leftovers of the many years he has worked as a director, he was interested to notice his last storyboards appeared to be better drawings. He and his family had moved three hours from Toronto on one of his early retirements and had experienced difficulties in slow communication times. Fax machines had been an early answer. Internet was better but drawings turned into minor messes and created confusion when clarity was needed. Clear storyboards had always been the director's best tool to explain how he wanted to do things, and so in the nineties, he began to draw everything with very simple lines and found they transmitted well. These Bell frames are a good example of images drawn with a minimum of lines. A useful method for those with a similar need.

Productions & Executions

Saintly Sequence

The director admired the courage of the Church of Jesus Christ of Latter Day Saints for stepping into the open and offering North Americans knowledge of the benefits of their faith system. Not only did they step out, they paid full price for a professional, commercial result. The faith system of the director's youth had been similar to the Latter Day Saints so he understood the needs of the LDS. The director no longer adhered to a faith system but the LDS had a good story and the director liked to tell a good story.

The Agency for the Church worked out of Salt Lake City, Utah. They were large, professional and enjoyed the benefit of good writers. The second job they sent the director was about a little girl who lived on a farm and decided to play in the family car even though she had been warned about the dangers. She bumped the gear shift lever as she pretended to corner and the car, now in neutral, began to roll backwards. Her little brother was on his tricycle near the car and when he saw the car move, he leapt off and ran to tell his mother. The car, now in full motion, just missed grandfather, erased the chicken coop, passed her older brother and the hired hand working on a pickup truck, and plopped rear-end first into the pond at the bottom of the hill. Mother arrived in full racing stride with tea-towel flying, just in time to see the car settle nose up to rear trunk level.

The logistics were the most interesting feature of the job. The budget made it a one day shoot, so it had to be shot like a documentary (takes were limited to three – visual perspectives were limited to two). This reality meant events had to work well the first time. When the director made a query about using two cameras, he was asked which camera he would like the cinematographer to light for. The other part of the same question was that when a second camera is required, the assistant cameraman is taken from the cameraman and given a second camera job.

This means the cameraman has to do the zoom and pull his own focus and that makes it more difficult to keep a good frame on a moving object. The shoot took its chances with one fully armed camera operated by a comfortable cameraman and busy assistant. The little girl was good and did her job well. The little boy looked like he had run off and squealed on someone before. When it came to the shot of the car's progress down the hill, the car had to be driven backwards by a man who was lying on the floor. The first shot was designed to miss the chicken coop, so the crew could save coop dramatics for a tighter shot. Great skill was required by the blind driver. He missed the coop but almost got the granddad and expertly came to a stop before the pond so we could do that as a close up with little girl in place. The best shot of the day was the eradication of the chicken coop. The car caught the corner of the coop with its right rear fender. *The car was a frequently repaired car used for film crashes.* Chickens and feathers filled the air and the coop, recognizing this as its moment of glory, flipped out a wall and executed a perfect pirouette as remaining parts settled in clouds of dust and feathers. For the last shot of the day, the little girl replaced the skilled, backward-driving driver in the driver's seat and did a good job pretending to be terrified as she drove backwards. To get the landscape to move past her in the correct direction, the car was placed backwards on a transport's low trailer that rolled forwards down a hill in the farm driveway. The crew, who finished before the sun set, agreed they could have done a good job if they had been asked to organize the Normandy landings. The spot continued as the little girl explained to her parents the escapade was her fault.
The viewer expects the father to reprimand his child. Instead he compliments her on her decision to tell the truth. And thereby an acceptable moral stance is presented to the public.

The director feels that the spots would have been better without moral underlines at the end. The director preaches that you should trust your viewer, honour his intelligence and he will return the honour by remembering what you have to say.

The director's favourite LDS commercial was his last. When the concept came in, the director called his favourite casting director and said, "Send me my favourite actor." His favourite actor was a pleasant looking fellow of normal appearance, who worked Second City and any other place he could squeeze a laugh from an audience. He wasn't gregarious. The casting director did a good job finding him. Listening to his endless monologue with the other performer was something we could have done all day long.

The performer was game and he was provided with a selection of attractive babies mounted in highchairs, that he was to feed and entertain. Babies have the same status as children under five. "No is no" and there is no possibility for accommodation. This means the process is to chat the baby up, work for a smile, or some sense your blather is getting through, offer a spoonful and see how many head movements, eye changes and expressions you can milk from the baby between spoonfuls. Soon all the babies are full and headed for a sound sleep and it's time to wake up the crew for lunch.

The script was invented by the performer as he went along and depended on what each baby gave him to work with. The performer was wonderful, as was the outcome.
The super at the end of the spot erased the need for moral underlines.

The super, after the baby's sneeze, read, "If you want your children to talk to you when they're older, talk to them when they're younger."

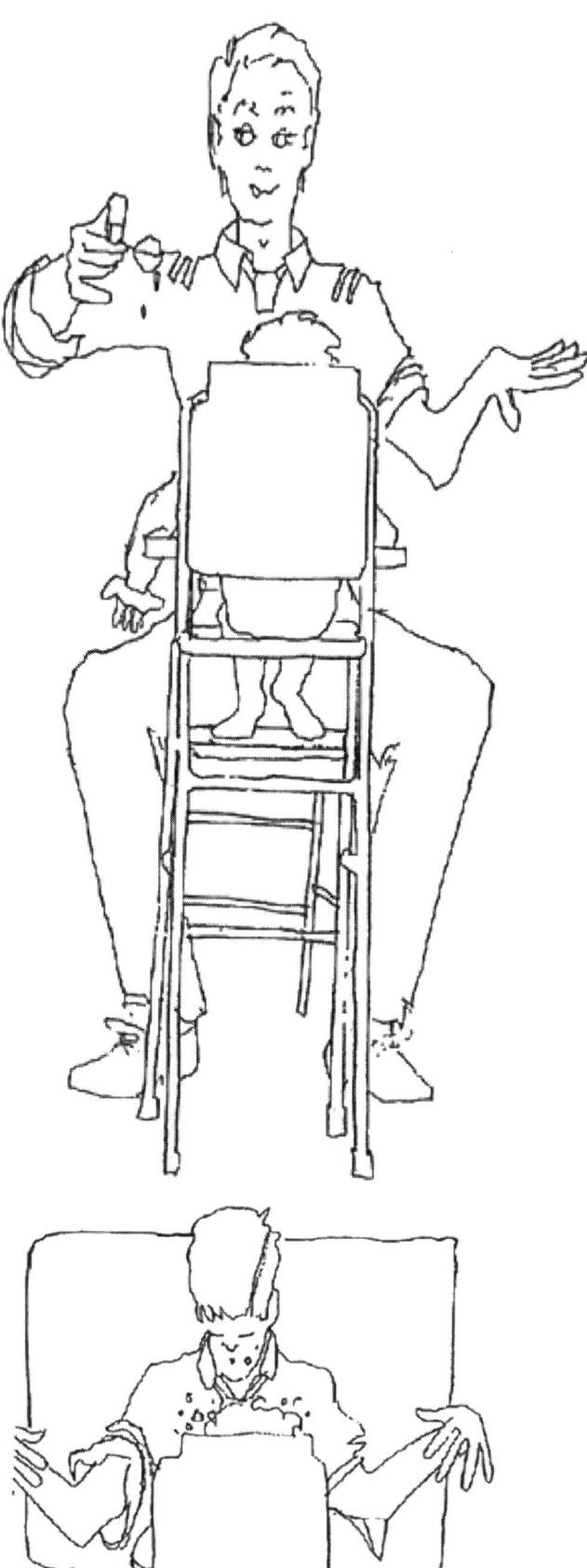

Productions
&Executions
Getting it Right

His parents were warm-blooded Belgians, his father, the famous Etretat and his mother Oekie. He was born in 1976 and during his short life he earned 1.5 million dollars, won two consecutive World Cups and many other prizes. He was inducted into the Hall of Fame and had a postage stamp made with his image on it. When he died at the age of twenty three, his local Chamber of Commerce erected a bronze statue in his honour.

I went to see him as he approached the end of his life. The Bank of Montreal was backing Big Ben and the fellow he gracefully carried on his back, for the world championships. They wanted a commercial to pump the donation and the event. Big Ben's home was just south of Perth, Ontario on county road one. A modest house is given an impressive backdrop by a pristine riding stable and large horse barn. Ben's owners were deep in the business of horses. Income was derived by training riders and jumpers, selling shares of competing jumpers, selling foals from pedigreed parents and sperm from a rig that simulated the mare's reproductive parts. Ben was not involved in this process; he had his maleness removed when he was younger, to better concentrate on his jumping. The idea strikes the director as an act similar to castrating male offspring to improve their scholastic focus.

Jumps were set up in a fenced area and the production unit shot the beautiful animal as Ben put on a show.

He kept his rider comfortably seated and in perfect position, never made the man-thing look unattached. He gracefully lowered his beautiful head so the man could see the jump ahead. The man touched him with heels and with the reins on his neck, but Ben didn't pay much attention. He'd been at this for years. There wasn't the usual big crowd and he didn't need reminders or suggestions for such a small event. His performance was swift, smooth and graceful.

The Bank of Montreal would be pleased. The horse seemed as able as the rider. The performance reminded the director of the day he watched the R.C.M.P. Musical Ride.

Two riders fell to the turf in the middle of the show but their horses completed the complex manoeuvres perfectly without their riders.

To add his own compliments to the magnificent Big Ben, the director walked to Ben's head, opened his own eyes wide and raised his chin. Ben's eyes opened wide and his head tilted in response, one ear flipped forward to acknowledge the visiting man-thing but the second ear never changed its focus. The second ear stayed turned to the rider, prepared and ever ready for the next command.

The person Ben carried so ably was Ian Millar, a quick and competitive animal of the human species. Big Ben and Mr. Millar won many international competitions together.

Productions &Executions

Mr. & Misses

There were commercials the other guy won the chance to do and the director wishes he'd had the opportunity to render them. There are storyboards that made him run away and spots came along that were worth begging for. Most of the people in our industry can be approached with an open mind and a few with whom it is a good idea to build a wall around. Some people make a spot better, some just make your day longer. Client-employed production advisors, more often than not failed producers, give advice to the disadvantage of their client. Production advisors are there with the purpose of ensuring monies are well spent and often drive the production budget to a level where a job of quality is not possible. Avoid them if you can. Give your executives training in film production. Then you have a person whose loyalties are with the company, not their pockets.

A storyboard came in for the director's treatment and he leapt at it like a rabid rabbit. Disney was suggesting they might use a Canadian production house for commercials to pump their new movie Mulan. The concept for the spot was delicious. A Mongol leader of heroic proportions hears the movie Mulan has gone to DVD. Fifty armoured warriors under his leadership rush out of the snowy plains and gallop into a modern city. The Mongol horses fill the street and stall traffic, as their leader marches into a video store to demand the DVD. A meek and diminished clerk mumbles that he is terribly sorry, the store doesn't have it yet. "Could you come back next week?" All fifty, mighty and muscled men adopt a downcast attitude and slowly move out of town, back towards the plain.

While working on a plauseable solution, the producer discovered there wasn't enough money to do it well. The money only covered ten armoured Mongol warriors. Their charge down the hill from the flat lands would have to be done with a master static shot and with the ten warriors making twelve trips down the hill, twenty feet apart. There goes half a day of shooting, on a one day shoot that has four more exteriors, one interior and a return up the hill. The director wonders if anyone ever shot it.

B.C.Tel sent some boards that were full of potential. The director was eager and drew many versions of how the stories could be told. In one of the spots, the company wanted to make their people look heroic as they struggled to put up a new line. The line ends at a cliff and a crew stands on the opposite and facing cliff, waiting for someone to figure out how to proceed. A strong young woman gets a bow and shoots a 'straw-line' across the gorge. The arrow sticks in a tree and the crew pulls the straw-line towards their side of the gorge. A telecommunication cable is attached to the straw-line and pulled to the other side. Problem solved.

The agency that handled B.C.Tel lost the creative director that wrote the commercial and the replacement creative demonstrated a severe lack of reason. The poor old director withdrew his services.

Latter Day Saints put out a call for commercial scripts and the director who had spent many years in Agency creative departments, dug out his pencils.

He wrote a quiet spot - it was of their genre. The director had found the locations he needed for it, walked in the creek to be certain of the depths and sat on the fence to make sure it would hold the two performers.

Nothing came of it and when the director asked for a reason, he was told the Church committee that approved scripts for production, had increased in size. The committee had originally been composed of twenty to thirty intelligent people. The committee had been increased to six hundred.

The commercial was about a father and daughter who went fishing and talked so much they never put a hook in the water.

Productions & Executions

Shooting Blind

It was Corn Flakes that took the director to Lake Rosseau in northern Ontario, to shoot in an exquisite, rustic cottage. The cottage sat on the top of a granite sheet. Where the sheet met the water, there was a direct ten foot drop to the lake. The cottage owner said he could get up in the morning, throw off his bed clothes and run off the cliff into the water, a morning plunge to start his day. The director preferred a coffee before his morning shower but didn't throw a question into the fellow's pleasures. The Corn Flakes commercial was one of two spots tested for the job he was about to shoot.

The one chosen was not the one the director thought would best attract viewers' interest. It was, however, the one that survived the diagnostic intricacies of the Kellogg's marketing masters. The spot with granddad won. The director liked the brothers who carted the Corn Flakes around in their wagon and had breakfast in bed wearing sunglasses. Which one would you have shot?

The intellectual precision of market research and testing may have sensors with which to read emotional attraction and understanding, the director doesn't know. Maybe the question underlines a double flaw; marketers need to have a greater knowledge of production and production needs to increase their knowledge of the sciences of marketing.

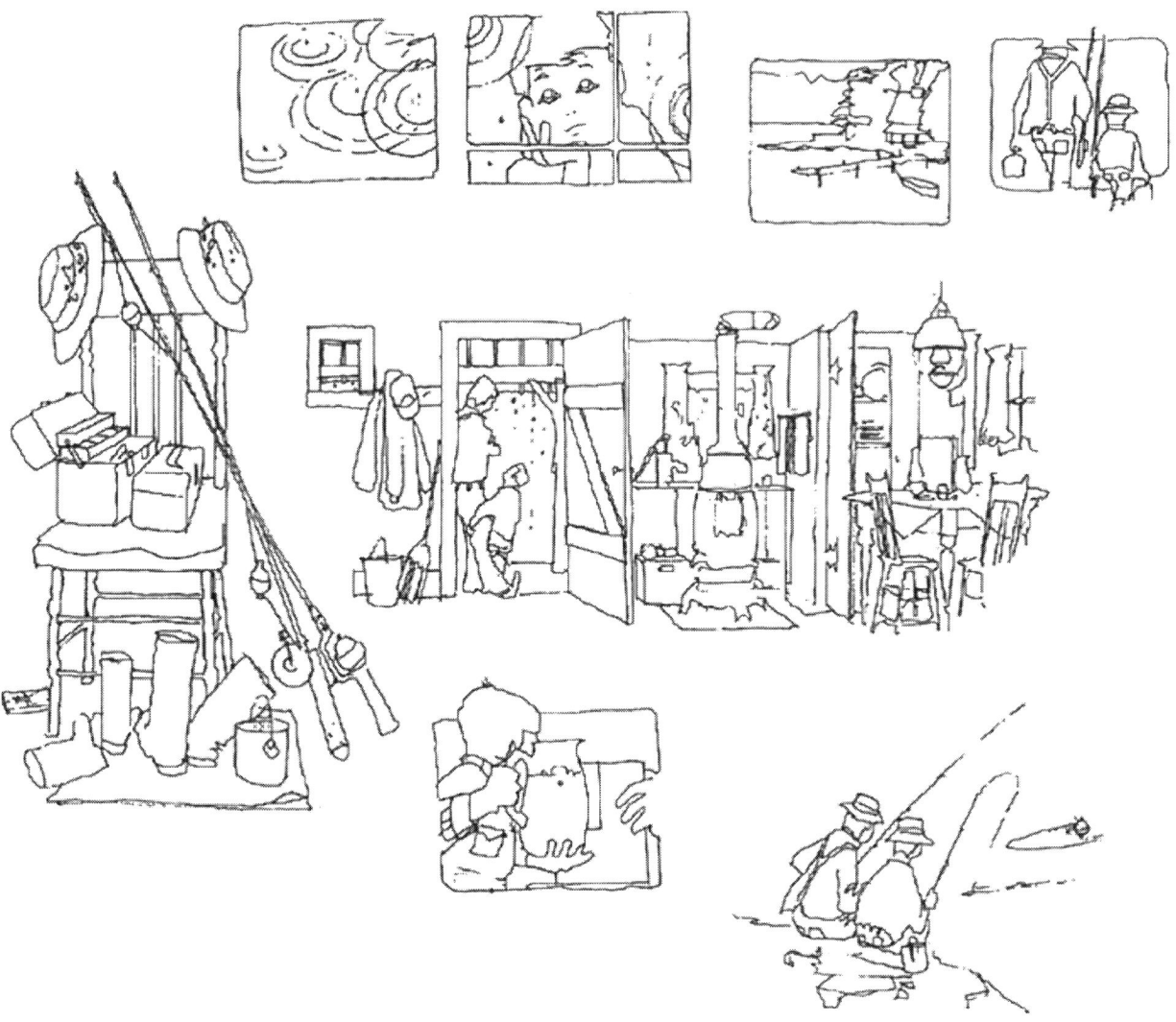

Productions &Executions

Russia - Part One

One of the incentives that pulled the future director towards his first experience with film, was an available job in a small studio whose impending project was to film in the Union of Soviet Socialist Republics.

It was 1969 and Air Canada would pay for the shoot because they had just inaugurated a new flight from Montreal to Moscow and they needed footage for use in an advertising campaign. Passports were required for future director and a demand that this junior fellow visit the U.S.S.R. embassy in Montreal. The answer to the director's question, "Why do they want to see me?" was straightforward, the answer oblique. "The K.G.B. want to question you." A flight to Montreal later, the junior director entered the front door of what appeared to be a normal residence on one of the streets beside Rue de Montagne. A polite woman asked whom he was there to see. He told her and she replied, "Ah, K.G.B." The woman suggested her guest sit in a specific chair and wait. Fifteen minutes later the K.G.B. Colonel arrived with a broad smile on a hand some face. "I don't think you are a spy, are you?" The two had an easy laugh and he thanked the junior director for coming to see him. Years later, a friend who had experience in diplomatic procedures explained the visit was not as innocent as it seemed. The specific chair was to accommodate a camera that viewed the potential visitor for a visual check. The fifteen minutes of waiting allowed the officer to check his sources for past misdemeanours and assess the level of unease in the subject.

The director flew to Moscow alone because the crew he was to join was already somewhere in the Caucasus Mountains. His instructions were to wait in the Moscow Hotel until he was given clear direction and a flight south was purchased for him. The day before he left Canada, the director was asked by a company named Visual Education Centre (VEC) to take a series of still photos to be compiled into educational strips for schools. He agreed and was given a letter of introduction under the letterhead of the company.

Half way to Moscow, the plane landed for fuel in Copenhagen. A gentle landing and the plane came to a halt at the landing port. The doors remained closed for longer than usual and when they opened, a spotless, diplomatic-type entered the aircraft. He took the loudspeaker from the wall and offered the surprising request, "Would Mr. Irish please come to the front of the aircraft?"

The junior director went forward and was taken to a private room where he was shown a telegram that read, "DO NOT - DO NOT - proceed to the Soviet Union without destroying V.E.C. letter!" The compliant air crew opened the belly of the plane and the director searched the luggage until he found his suitcase and destroyed the letter.

The Copenhagen incident remained a mystery for him until he returned to Canada . Apparently, the evening before he boarded the plane, an unexpected delivery of smuggled film of the Hungarian uprising, had arrived unexpectedly at V.E.C. On the night the junior director lifted into the air, the owner of the education company had a sudden image of the poor fellow bound for Siberia and a KGB prison because he was a spy connected to a company called V.E.C. that received covert material.

Russia - Part Two

On touch down at the Moscow airport, the director's concerns were augmented by the sight of soldiers with machine guns across their chests. They lined the walkways and were omnipresent in the terminal. He took a cab to the Moscow Hotel in the centre of the city. The cabbie got out and went to the back of the car to get the director's suitcase. The director also dismounted and went around to take the suitcase. When he reached for it, the cabbie didn't release the case. Instead, he leaned forward to whisper in the director's ear, "No talk this hotel, people listen." After a healthy tip to the cabbie, the director signed in and was given a spacious nineteenth century corner room. He had a thousand questions and he hoped, a few days freedom in a country he never thought he would have a chance to see. Big Brother or not, he was impressed with his introduction to the film business. He grabbed his stills camera and was off, clicking away at everything in sight.

At that time (1969), half of the Moskovites listened to the BBC and therefore spoke English with a British accent. The other half listened to Air America and spoke with an American accent. The director was stopped on the street by a little fellow, perhaps eight, who asked politely in a British accent for the time. The director answered and the boy said, "Just practising" with an engaging smile. Next, an attractive young woman wanted to buy his pants. He was a little taken aback until she explained with an American accent that jeans were very popular but not for sale in Russian stores. His hotel was very close to Red Square. Two boundaries of Red Square were the Cathedral of St. Basil and the wall of the Kremlin that held Lenin's Tomb. The square itself seemed a square mile of cobblestone. A fierce looking Russian soldier stopped the director and tried to tell him something about his feet. He wondered if the soldier wanted to buy his shoes but eventually understood that he was standing on a stone in the cobblestone square that he should not be standing on. He quickly stepped off the slightly larger stone and assumed he had been the brunt of a joke. He learned later the larger stone had an ugly history.

In 1853, the imperious Russian Emperor, Ivan the Terrible, lined up his subjects below the Kremlin wall in order to address them. His subjects stood with their heads bowed and if anyone raised their head to meet his eyes, the penalty was beheading. The director had been standing on Ivan's bloody, beheading stone. Legend has it that Ivan the Terrible was hugely pleased with an architect who designed a beautiful and elaborate church for his use. He was so concerned the architect might design another even more beautiful church for someone else, he had the architect's eyes put out.

There were several other 'Ivans' in Russian history - Ivan the Fair, Ivan the Great and even a fellow named Ivan the Moneybag.

Freedom to wander was soon curtailed. A message arrived that he was to catch a flight south to Sochi on the Black Sea and meet with the film crew. The film crew consisted of cameraman, Russian producer, Intourist guide, and soundman. The director had been shown how to use the Nagra recorder and was upgraded to soundman. The first subject was a gypsy musician in the high mountains behind Sochi. We left in the morning and arrived close to lunch time at a structure that looked a great deal like a fort from a western movie. The wall that surrounded a group of wooden buildings was made of vertical logs all carefully pointed at the top. The gypsy musician was a regular performer at what turned out to be a tourist restaurant. In the USSR, everyone was unionized and holidays were gifted to the workers after a prescribed number of work days. Sochi was one of the many resort towns where the workers enjoyed their holiday. The gypsy was to arrive just after sunset. The crew used the time to build a bonfire and set up lights in front of the restaurant. The sun set, the gypsy arrived, the fire raged and the camera rolled. Halfway through the man's sad song about his mother, while his golden tooth glinted and tears poured down his cheeks, the lights went out. Outside the circle of the fire, no one could see past the end of their noses. The crew felt their way to the cars, dragging what equipment they could, when they realized their Russian producer was not with them.

Joining arms, the crew stumbled through the area where they had been working. Eventually someone said, "Quiet" and everyone was aware of the sound of sobbing. Our young Russian producer, Sasha, was a student of the Moscow Film Centre and his heart was broken because he felt it was his fault the lights had gone out and he had let us down. The next morning, everyone was wakened by police and told to go to the beach. Obediently, we set out for the beach somewhat apprehensive of what was about to take place.

A man in a rumpled suit accompanied by a woman with two small children was brought down and bruskly pushed into place in front of us. The policeman explained that this was the man who had turned out the lights and asked what we wanted done with the family. We asked if they would tell us why the lights were turned out. The man explained that the workers in the restaurant had gathered at the windows to watch what we were doing and were not cleaning up after the evening's business. The manager had a fixed budget and the only way he could get his workers back to their chores was to turn out the lights. We explained that we understood his dilemma and asked that he not be penalized. At breakfast, we ate with a thought appropriate to the times - that we had perhaps saved the young family from the Gulag.

Russia - Part Three

Having finished with our subjects in Sochi, the team climbed into a couple of cars and headed south and east through the Caucasian Mountains, past the eastern borders with Turkey and into the state of

Georgia. Our destination was Tblisi, the capital city of Georgia. Here we had two projects, one for the film crew and one for the acting stills photographer/ sound man/ director.

Tblisi is situated in a deep valley and sits on the confluence of ancient trade routes. The city's position made it vulnerable to roving armies. From the time of Genghis Khan, the city has been razed to the ground, and rebuilt forty times. From the director's hotel window, he looked down on a four story building whose stages of reconstruction could be seen in the layers of the different building materials that climbed its walls.

Water poured from the height of land above Tblisi, in a huge silver pipe. Where the pipe ended in the valley below, a large fountain threw the water into the air to aerate it.

The city officials chose this open area around the fountain as the location for the filming of a favourite and traditional Georgian dance. Georgian men are more masculine in appearance than other male members of the human race. The women appear consistently handsome and capable. The dance began with the symbolic dropping of a woman's lace handkerchief and ended with a mighty swirling and clanging of swords. The dance told the story of conflict over a young woman's love. What better reason do men have to flail about with deadly weapons?

While the crew was preparing to move on, the director went to visit a local artist by the name of Goba Gueruli.

The residents of Tblisi speak three languages, Russian, Georgian and an ancient language, written in an Arabic script. During the interview, he spoke the ancient language and a woman translated it to Russian. The Intourist guide understood and a second translator flipped Russian to English, so the director could understand. While this slow tangle of interpretations was going on, everyone drank Georgian champagne and slurped thick slices of local watermelon.

Goba was obviously employed by the State, but he was a charmer and entertained his guests with style and grace. His art consisted ot hammered copper sheets that held images of the Georgian countryside, its features and local livestock.

Russia - Part Four

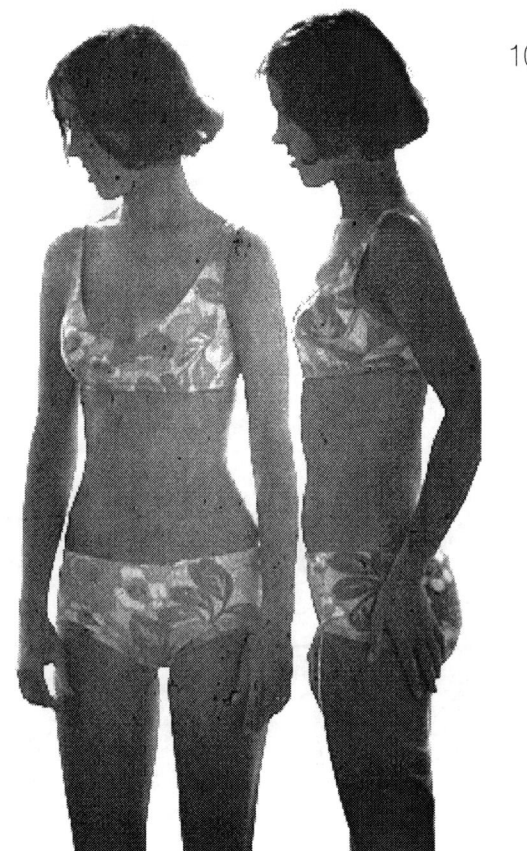

Finished with Tblisi and the State of Georgia, we drove the four hundred miles back through the Caucasus to Sochi airport and got on a plane.

The Sochi to Kiev aircraft looked like a *1945 DC-3*. The seats were better than the other more modern aircraft but the whole thing had the atmosphere of a crowded bus. The temperature on the tarmac was over 100 degrees. A man with a bristle broom walked the wings. Our seating arrangement was three passengers facing a table with three others on the opposite side. The three other passengers were Russian soldiers.

The wait on the tarmac ended when the female pilot and co-pilot climbed on board. The fellow with the broom flipped to the ground and the flying oven lurched into the air. At a higher elevation, the co-pilot pulled a lever and a row of vents on the roof opened, shooting plumes of cold air into the cabin. It was a signal many had been waiting for because men filled the aisle, ripped open their shirts and pointed their hairy chests at the plumes of air. Immune to the smell of perspiration, the director fell asleep and woke in a light rain. Droplets fell lightly from the cabin roof as the cold air took the humidity out of the 100 degree heat.

As the director closed his eyes again, he noticed that the soldier who sat on the right side across from him was carefully removing the leather belt from the sleeping soldier who sat in the middle. As the soldier slid the last length of the belt from the pant loops, he winked, folded the belt and slipped it into the third soldier's carry-on.

Before leaving Kiev, we took a singing group to a beach and filmed as they sang and frolicked in the water.

Kiev was interesting for its place in early history and the intricate design of its ninth century Russian Orthodox churches. The Dnieper River ran through the city, giving the Ukraine access to the Mediterranean through the Black Sea. The ground floor windows of the large buildings were surrounded by unrepaired shell holes from WWII military engagements.

It was impossible not to admire the Russian attitudes of the time towards the value of women. One of the twin vocalists in the singing group was a graduate mechanical engineer, the other a designer of aeronautic structures. Our last job was to shoot a walled monastery with a history that predated most of the surrounding towns and villages. As had happened in many places in the USSR, the generous community decided to feed us in traditional style. A monk's dinner of an ancient recipe of potato stew and potato beer was served on unpainted wooden tables covered in white cloths. It was almost as intoxicating as the twin sisters who sang at the beach.

Russia – Part Five

The director/sound man/stills photographer returned to Moscow with the crew and the crew was enhanced by the arrival of the cameraman's wife. We were then given an Intourist guide named Luba to show us what to shoot and what not to shoot in the capital city. We shot a dance troupe in the gardens of the palatial home where Rasputin, the Tsarina's religious advisor, was poisoned. The Volga River ran by below the elaborate gardens, on its winding way to the sea. The shoot was distinctive in the fact that the amount of film exposed, and the minutes of sunshine, matched exactly.

The day after the dance troupe, the crew was taken to an important religious capital in the time of the Tsars named Suzdal. Seen from a distance, Suzdal was a tiny village wearing forty onion domed helmets, all pointing skyward. The Tsar used the town for his religious worship, making frequent trips to the exquisite and icon filled structures.

The trip was interesting. Luba sat in the front seat with her driver. The cameraman, his wife and the director sat in the back seat. About half way to Suzdal, the cameraman's wife expressed her need to use a bathroom. When the vehicle floated through the next village without stopping, she asked again. Another few miles without stopping, put the woman in dire straits. She asked the driver to stop so she could use the roadside bushes. Still there was no change in the pace of the vehicle. She looked to her husband who was a man of considerable size and strength. He leaned forward, grasped the necks of Luba and her driver and lifted them off their seats and demanded the car stop immediately. The car stopped and the lady rushed off into the bushes. Luba was furious. She screamed at her driver for making the stop and threw loud accusations into the back seat.

Our group was apparently ill mannered and without respect for Russian rules. She sank into silence until her driver, seeing it as his turn, chose to disobey. Luba exploded as the the car slowed to exit the two-laned road. She screamed, spit and threw epithets at her driver at the top of her lungs.

Did I mention Luba was a tiny person?

The courageous driver seemed oblivious to the abuse and continued his turn off the road. We had turned into a tiny town. At the main intersection was a farm truck with a van-sized wooden barrel sitting in the back. Our driver, to a noisy background of Luba expletives, got out, talked to the man at the truck, then filled five glass tankards with a locally crushed fruit drink. He returned to the car and handed them around. Again under Luba's loud vocal distress, he explained in stumbled English. "Sorry, road watched, trip timed. Sorry." Once again the ordinary Russian showed he cared while the bureaucracy proved it didn't. The drink put out Luba's fire but her mood and her sullen posture didn't improve for several days.

The remainder of the trip was uneventful but allowed us to see that each of the wooden homes along the road to Suzdal had its front walls freshly painted for tourism. However, the sides and backs were left in more attractive weathered wood. We were later told by another guide that the road to Suzdal skirted sensitive areas and had six checkpoints at intervals along the way. A car with other than Russian occupants was expected to travel at a specific speed and pass through each of the points at a specified time. Poor Luba.

Russia – Last Part

The novice director's first practical experience with film was endlessly interesting and gifted him with a lasting affection for the people of the Soviet Union.

The month in the U.S.S.R. was exhilarating. The director had lived something few people would have the opportunity to experience.
His mind was filled with memories, his socks with souvenir rubles and his arms loaded with boxes of film.

In his exuberance, he got carried away and waved goodbye to a soldier with a rifle across his chest. He didn't get a response. The director was lifted into the air with a broad smile and a bottle of cold Air Canada milk in each hand.
At that time, Russians did not eat corn, cut their grass or have pasteurized milk. Visitors therefore who were accustomed to milk found it not available.

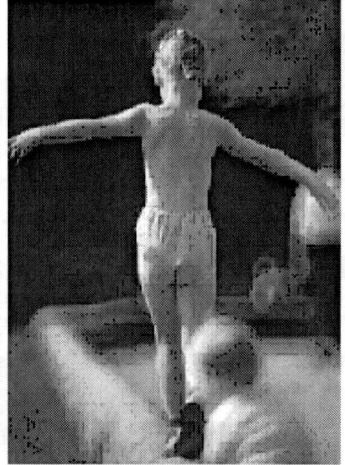

William (Bill) Irish is an experienced
art director, film director, writer,
illustrator and graphic designer.

Now retired from fifty years of work
in advertising and film he enjoys
free-lance work and private projects.

Bill holds a "Lifetime of Excellence
in the field of Communication Award"
from the Toronto Art Directors Club
and several awards from the
Canadian Television Bureau for
his work in film.

This book is his attempt to give a
step up to anyone who would like
to work in film.

Enjoy

CPSIA information can be obtained at www.ICGtesting.com
Printed in the USA
LVOW09*0709120515

438117LV00010B/94/P